SCOTLAND

*à **Malo, mon petit-fils.***

Malo, disciple et fidèle compagnon de Brendan,
le Saint Navigateur, dont les rapports de mer
m'encouragèrent à aller a-delà de mes horizons bretons

Philip PLISSON

Published for the first time in the UK by Octopus Publishing Group 2003.

PATRICK MAHÉ • PHILIP PLISSON ⚓

SCOTLAND

Translated into English by
VIVIANE VAGH and JONATHAN LEVINE

To Eric Tabarly

They had decided to meet up in Scotland...For the two French sailors from Brittany (Eric Tabarly and Philip Plisson), the sea is what bonds the Celtic world together. The Iroise Currents, the rocks of Cornouailles in Brittany, France, the cliffs of Ireland and the mocking puffins around the Gaelic Islands is the common bond that forms the collective Celtic memory, a world united by common legends and music.

Eric Tabarly knew those strewn Celtic coasts well...ports, harbors and sea sides. He had discovered Scottish sea shanties in Glasgow, rediscovered their Irish flavor in Cork and brought back these same sailor's songs to Concarneau (Brittany, France). He knew everything about the ocean mists, the turning winds, the white suns of the north, the fraternal beacons and the rays of the lighthouses guiding his sail on moonless nights.

Philip Plisson, a photographer fishing for images, his shoulder bag full of beautiful photos, had described to Tabarly the Scotland he wanted to capture in photos from out at sea. Together, they'd make a great team. Everyone has heard about the austere beauty of the Highlands, the mountains and valleys, the salmon rivers, whiskey and the village pubs along the banks, like oases. Ringing bagpipes, colored tartans, arm-wrestling, titanic sports, fishing, hunting and golf, make a universal theme for photo albums "made in Scotland." Every image in Scotland has already been taken before. Except for images of Scotland from out at sea!

This is where Philip Plisson comes in. His new way of looking at Scotland brings a new perspective to an old subject.

Philip had spoken to Eric about the project – *Scotland* – two years before during the big maritime exhibition, "Brest 96." They had dined with their families aboard Philip's boat, *Pêcheur d'Images*, a 13 meter (42.6 feet) trawler.

Together, they had spread out their sea maps. Philip had thought of an ideal route, by way of the Hebrides scattered around the west coast and then up to the Orkneys nestled in the waters of the Great North.

Tabarly spoke knowingly about Scotland yet he always remained modest and reserved. He loved to talk about Fairlie as a famous place for yacht building. Fairlie is majestically camped on the Clyde, a saltwater river that winds up to Glasgow. The Fife Dynasty had established its headquarters for naval architecture on its banks. How many fine racing sailing boats, all slender like white swans, had been built there? *Pen Duick*, Tabarly's boat, was designed by William Fife III, a renowned figure of Scotland and the Clyde. He had drawn this sensual and vivid work of art. "A cutter," he said, admiring the way it cut through the water like a blade. An Irish shipyard had launched it. This was in 1898.

Tabarly had accepted to celebrate the centenary of this masterpiece, on the spot where it had been conceived and built. At Fairlie.

Plisson dreamt of going there, too. It would be heaven to

TO THE LEFT

Patrick Mahé and Philip Plisson

TO THE RIGHT

Marie-Brigitte Plisson and
Antonia Small, nicknamed Tony.

have both Scotland and *Pen Duick*. As a child, he was overwhelmed by the nautical ballet in the harbor of Trinité-sur-Mer (Brittany) during the *Gwenn ha du* festival (named after the black and white Brittany flag). *Pen Duick* moved with the grace of a swallow skimming on the water, high sails guiding the foresail and the fore staysail, like the plumage of a great bird. It had the spirit of a sea bird. The name *Pen Duick* comes from the Breton *duin* (to blacken) and *glaouig* (head of a bluebird).

Plisson, our photographer, would later savor the privilege of being welcomed aboard the boat of France's greatest ocean racer. Jacqueline Tabarly and Marie-Brigitte Plisson (their wives) had become close friends.

Unforeseen changes in their schedule had changed their Scottish meeting into a rendezvous that would never take place.

Philip Plisson was coming back from Fairlie, his shoulder bag full of photos for this book. Eric Tabarly was running for his Royal Jubilee, his head up in the stars. He would never get there. His tragic end threw a black veil over the Celtic sea.

But, he is here, floating on these pages. This Scotland from the sea signed Plisson is naturally, also his.

Patrick Mahé

Eric Tabarly aboard Pen Duick.

All sails swollen with strength and pride, the *H.M.S. Rose* speeds through the ocean towards Ireland. At the extreme northwest of the coastline one makes out the outlines of vestiges of the ancient mission where St. Colomba brought his monks to convert Scotland. This was in the sixth century. The boat, a three-masted American, starred banner in the stern, sails around Malin Head, on the tip of Ulster. Soon it will cross the Giant's Causeway. This natural site has been classified as one of the wonders of World Patrimony since 1987. Waves crash in bouquets against the regimented alignment of 37,000 columns formed by rock called the Giant's Causeway. The rumbling water and the hissing winds makes these basaltic organs look even more grandiose.

Camped up on the stern, Tony, a flaming blonde with clear blue eyes, savors the last miles of the crossing. It was as though a marine opera was saluting this cathedral made of sails (the *H.M.S. Rose*).

Like Tony, 60 million Americans are of Irish origin. 40 million have Scottish descent. Half of the population of the United States can claim Celtic descent. They are the children of the Great Famine which pulled a black veil over the Emerald Isle. They are also the children of the Clearances of Scotland which massively expelled Highlanders at the dawn of the Culloden Defeat (In 1746, the victorious English chased the sons of the defeated Clans out of their mountains and valleys, replacing them with intensive sheep breeding).

In Ireland, they escaped from Derry, Belfast and Dublin. Here in Scotland, from Edinburgh, Inverness, Aberdeen and Glasgow…

They live in the United States and Canada. They landed, to save themselves, on lands that needed to be tamed and built up. They have made Australia and New Zealand.

Two centuries later, their hearts are on their sleeves. Inconsolable tears fall, when on St. Andrews Day, patron of Scotland, bagpipes ring out, "Amazing Grace," or when on St. Patrick's Day, patron of Ireland, "Molly Malone" (muse of the pubs) is sung (Molly was the young fishmonger who died during the great fevers) and whiskey, the *eau-de-vie* of Celtic peoples, their water (*eau*) of survival, is drunk.

The Celts cultivate their past, like the wise men of Asia or the Indian tribes

who perpetuate their oral legends and religion.

On this day, day and night, Celts wistfully talk about their family trees and nostalgically dream of a trip back all together. Celtic blues…

O'Brien from Sydney or from Chicago will always find an Irish cousin on the road to Tipperary…Mackinnon, from Auckland or from Chicago, will dream of the proud descendants of Stirling or of the Isle of Skye, where Bonnie Prince Charlie, the last Pretender to the Scottish Throne, and Flora MacDonald, the Highland's heroine, sank before banishment and exile.

They are thousands. They are millions. Tony is alone. She has chosen this ocean route. She comes from Boston and lives in New York. With scarcely any personal belongings, she embarked at Bridgeport in Connecticut, the home port of the *H.M.S. Rose*. She sails up the Atlantic against the winds of history. Against the current. For her, New Scotland (Nova Scotia), already in the distance is nothing like the Canadian Island of the same name facing Quebec. This New Scotland is truly the old land of the great ancestors…of Robert Bruce, Rob Roy, and William Wallace, *Braveheart* revisited.

A land bordered by the sea. A nurturing sea at that! Under the breaking waves, squadrons of fish are caught by non-industrial fishermen in this maritime Eden. These treasures were abandoned after military and rural England had laid their hands on the country. Navigation was forbidden…Today, oil is drilled in the North Sea from platforms along the string of little islands. The providential black gold is an important part of the new prosperity that is opening up to Scotland in the third millennium. It's giving Scotland back part of its sovereignty.

Tomorrow, the *Saltire* (the Scottish flag with the white cross on a blue background), will fly over the reestablished Parliament in Edinburgh. Forever and again new Scotland is being reborn amongst secular traditions and renewed modernity.

It is in this Scotland, opened onto tomorrow, that Philip Plisson meets up with Tony, witnesses today and remembers yesterday. He is a photographer who can be proud of the honor of being the official Marine painter. He has anchored his boat to better focus his lens on this nation in evolution. This is where he looks out for the *H.M.S. Rose*, a replica of the original ship with many historical conquests. It's here that Tony will embark on his boat.

The Loch Long, on the right bank of the Clyde.

Inveraray on the right bank of Loch Fyne and the home of the Campbell Clan.

Beacons on the Clyde by Gourock.

Glasgow has inherited the boldness of Victorian architecture.

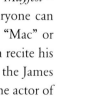

Glasgow is a town that swings, that rocks and rolls, turns and tangos. Especially on Saturdays when football is king in town. It's impossible to escape the fever which has, for the last 110 years, opposed the green of Celtic to the blue of Rangers, and which is now played out four times a year in the League alone.

Today, on the south side of the river, at Ibrox Park, in the Govan neighborhood, passions are high as the "Gers" are playing at home to the "Bhoys". Another day will see a return at Parkhead, and so it goes and goes. Celtic *v.* Rangers and Rangers *v.* Celtic is Glasgow's big challenge! These conflicts also perpetuate the myth about a place which once went from a glorious past as Second City of the British Empire to the decay of the post-Industrial era. But nowadays there's more to Glasgow than meets the eye.

Being named the European Cultural Capital in 1990 gave Glasgow a lift. When Philip Plisson docked there in spring, he experienced the atmosphere of the new artistic festival – *the Mayfest* – where creative popular imagination was everywhere. Everyone can have their own show there, for better or for worse. Any "Mac" or "Jimmy" (a popular name to the average Glaswegian), can recite his poem inspired by Robert Burns' odes to whiskey or play the James Bond of the neighborhood. For a day, for an hour, he is the actor of his own show, champion of his street, idol for a night, in a town transformed into an everyman's theater. For three weeks, the bars stay open day and night. Everywhere tavern bands perform amidst

rounds of draft beer bought by their friends.

Therefore, Glasgow, the black city on black waters, becomes green again, finding vitality, creative youth and its Celtic roots. *Glas Cu* or *Clas-lu* means dear green space in Gaelic.

This is a city of a hundred parks. The main one is Glasgow Green where the bagpipers make you feel nostalgic shivers for only a few coins or blue pound notes on which "Bank of Scotland" is proudly printed today. Then comes Kibble Palace, decorated with Victorian steel. They both give the smoke-filled lungs of the old city a tropical scent from the plants that were brought back from Asia, South Africa and the Americas. Also to the north are the hills of Kelvingrove Park, a crown of greenery, where the university campus is located. In the south, duck ponds and play areas where redheaded youths fly and slalom on their skateboards between the menhirs and the dolmens scattered here and there.

Green city and city of art. Mainly, its boldness comes from the avant-garde architect Charles Rennie Mackintosh, who approached the twentieth century as a pioneer of art nouveau.

He designed the Kate Cranston tea rooms. There is only one left out of the original four. He also designed their styled interiors, furniture, tables, high chairs and even the silverware. He was an inspired dandy who wore a curled up moustache and a perpetually dishevelled bow tie and challenged Victorian classicism. His opening of large spaces, his use of pure Asian lines, especially Japanese, made this Scotsman a born universal creator. He changed the outmoded approach of the builders of this austere and somber city. If the whole of Glasgow resembled the central station, an immense greenhouse of wood, glass and steel, or resembled his art school, a fortress of light, the rain and the winds that gust through Glasgow's

frozen alleys would be forgotten.

Today, Glasgow's renovation, neighborhood by neighborhood, street by street, has already given it color. Glasgow is becoming a beauty. Everything has developed: cinema, rock, theater. There is life again. Gone is the time, when the disdainful traveller nostalgic for the sea or the Highlands avoided going there so that they wouldn't see the sad-looking city. Blessed be Mungo, patron saint of the town, fifteen centuries after his burial – he rests in the gardens of the medieval cathedral – Glasgow has again become the *Glas Cu* of his first visions.

Even the River Clyde is no longer a black river clouded with white smoke and bordered by its sinister Red Road Flats. These red brick towers of the southern suburbs dominate the uniform alignments of working class houses and the old slums where typhoid and cholera spread in the past.

Philip continues his way between two rows of quasi-abandoned docks. Today, some have been transformed into pedestrian zones, others into shopping malls. A lot of the working class people have built these places themselves. Up until then, what had given them hope was a kind of proletarian quest for a grail which would release them and give them a better social status. This same working class would be intoxicated by the fairy-tale spectacle of these majestic buildings that look like sailboats, built by their own hands, like the four masted *North* – a building of one hundred meters high (328 feet), with a six thousand square meter façade – religiously constructed in 1889. Its tallest mast reaches sixty meters (197 feet) high.

Where laborers once toiled to build the *Queen Mary* and the *Queen Elizabeth* ocean liners, there are now renovated workshops between rusted warehouses. Talented designers have transformed

For the last ten years, Glasgow has shifted its past into the present. In 1990, the town receives the title "European City of Culture."

Central Station, a mixture of glass and steel in the Victorian style.

them into high-priced lofts. Here, boats are docked. There, ferries are being reconstructed. People working everywhere. It's like a renaissance. Glasgow which was relegated to the past and was losing twenty thousand inhabitants a year in the 1960s, has regained its foothold and is becoming a trendy place.

*At Port Glasgow,
Newark Castle is surrounded
by shipyards for
medium-sized ships.*

*Dumbarton Castle.
It's here that Mary Queen
of Scots sailed for France
in 1548.*

The banks of the Clyde hold many treasures…the waterfalls of Cora Linn and its millers' village, Chatelherault Palace, heritage of the *Auld Alliance* – the old royal Franco-Scottish pact of 1295, is still remembered here – and especially Dumbarton Castle.

Dumbarton Castle is where Mary Queen of Scots, daughter of James II and Mary of Guise, was crowned at her baptism and embarked for France in 1548. She was then five years old and was already very lively. The little girl entertained the whole crossing and set the example to the other children of noble families. Catholicism of French influence was getting weaker. The Reform and the ultra-Calvinist preaching of John Knox was enflaming the spirits. The Channel was constellated with English boats ready for battle. One had to sail way out at sea to avoid them.

Philip can't help thinking about Mary when he reaches Dumbarton Castle. This huge square manor looks even bigger when it's reflected in the water. Imagination does the rest. It takes us back to the tragic destiny of little Mary. Imagine her as a child, happy and all dressed up in the arms of Henry II's oldest son, on her glorious day at Notre Dame. She was fifteen and the dauphin, fourteen when amid deep organ sounds and choir, Scotland and France were united

before God in Paris. A year later, Francis II was on the throne. At 16, Mary, Queen of Scotland (by birth), also became Queen of France. Another year later Francois died traveling between Chambord, Saint-Germain and Fontainebleau. Mary came back to Scotland dressed in black. She was only 18. A little later, England would have her head. It would roll in wood shavings under the axe of the executioner.

Goodbye Dumbarton, to Mary, her black and graceful ghost. Philip's trawler, named *Pêcheur d'Images*, sails on the Firth of Clyde. It looks like a gulf. The Gulf of Morbihan except four or five times larger with its peaceful waters but also its counter currents. Full of little islands like vessels, its waters turning into a deep blue as Philip goes further and further out to sea. The huge merchant fleet, the pride of the British Empire – Brittania Rules the Waves – had sailed between these islands. The mainland bordered by fishing villages hides modern and happy summer resorts. Modern Glasgow has its beaches. Every pier is a rest stop where the sailor of a day crosses the lifelong sailor. They wave to one another. When night falls, they look at the sky together. "It was a nice day," they say, and they nostalgically close up the day beach to go into a quiet evening: "Have a nice night, see you tomorrow."

You can treat yourself to a month of, half river half maritime, sailing on the Firth of Clyde. To the villages of Greenock, Helensburgh or to a little vacation on the lochs, these stretches of sea that flow between rocks and forests, call out to seasonal holiday makers.

Dunoon is the cultural center. Its solemn parade of bagpipers and its traditional games attract a big crowd during the month

ABOVE LEFT

A small steam tugboat on the Clyde.

ABOVE RIGHT

For the traffic on the Clyde, because of shallow waters, there's a need for considerable beaconing.

OPPOSITE

In the nineteenth century, Glasgow and the banks of the Clyde were home to the biggest naval shipyards in the world.

RIGHT

In the nineteenth century, Glasgow and the banks of the Clyde was the home of the largest shipyards in the world.

ABOVE

In 1832, the Scottish bagpipes started being used in Brittany.

BELOW RIGHT

On the top of the bell tower of Fairlie, the weather vane represents a yawl. It is on the banks of the Clyde River, in the village of Fairlie, that generations of Fifes conceived, amongst other ships, **Shamrock I** *and* **Shamrock III** *for Sir Thomas Lipton and* **Pen Duick** *for Eric Tabarly.*

of August. Rothesay, on the neighboring isle of Bute, competes to attract holiday makers. Rothesay is the last promontory on the banks of the Clyde. *Pêcheurs d'Images*, Philip's boat, drops anchor there. Here in the past, a wood fire was lit in place of a lighthouse. Stuarts Castle has guarded the vast entrance since the eighteenth century. Even the Vikings sailed on these seas.

Scotland has three hundred historical sites: castles, fortresses, medieval towers, abbeys, Druid stones, etc. These all make the trip fascinating. All the way up to Cumbrae Island (that opens up on to the Isle of Arran), aquariums, museums and botanical gardens, flourish like the heather on the hills.

The Clyde Tower is a poignant historical stop where sailors remember and dream under star-filled skies. Fairlie is only a small port. Cumbrae Island blocks the view of the opposite bank on Bute, therefore on Rothesay. This is the crossroad of navigation's heyday. The wrecks of ships decay in front of the nuclear submarine base of Cove and near shipyards for luxury yachts.

This is where the most beautiful drawings of maritime architecture have been done. The Fife Family has drawn the most beautiful yachts, the majority have come out of the construction sites of Fairlie. *Shamrock*, *Shamrock I* (in 1897), *Shamrock III* (in 1903), jewels of the first America styles. *Pen Duick*, constructed in Ireland, was also a child of that family. A Fife design. In honor of our friend Tabarly, the man of *Pen Duick*, a reproduction of a yawl, a two-masted sailing boat, was created under the bell tower of Fairlie.

Thomas Lipton, child of Glasgow, dreamt of these famous marine masterpieces signed William Fife. He had to wait many tides before he was admitted into the circle of the small aristocracy of the

Royal Clyde Yacht Club. It's there, before becoming a figure of yachting, and a peer of the kingdom by Queen Victoria in 1898, that the Emperor of Tea with the big moustache, posed for posterity. He had challenged the America Cup five times. Wearing his famous white cap with the black brim, "Sir Tea," entered into the legend of the sea.

The Largs Marina, a few miles away, can berth a thousand boats. Philip's trawler is immediately given a spot to dock.

The welcome is warm from the captain down to the last worker in the pub:

"Are you French?"

"Yes."

"Oh, France, our old ally."

"You fly Breton flags…"

"Yes, Gwenn ha du."

"Ah! Brittany, our Celtic sister…"

"Slainté! To your health!"

The red beer glasses clink and backed by a harmonica, the deep voice of a shanty singer sings a typical Scottish song. Philip, wearing a Scottish woolen marine bonnet, with a red pompom, readily lifts his glass. He offers the next round. There will be others…

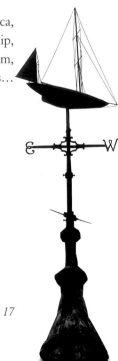

*"Miniature Scotland," this is how
Arran Isle is described on the
Clyde Estuary.*

*Three mountaintops that reach more than 800 meters
(2,624 feet) in the north of Arran Isle create spectacular
waterfalls because of heavy rains.*

*After tourism, the main source
of income of Arran Isle comes from
breeding and agriculture.*

Off to the Isle of Arran. This is a miniature of Scotland, a hundred meters (328 feet) of coast, bathed in sunlight. Philip Plisson sails entirely around it, anchors in the bay of Lamlash then at Brodick under the red stone Castle.

There are a lot of things to see on Arran. Impressive circles with stones brought up to Machrie Moor in the south which were probably laid there in 1600 BC. White cliffs and mountains of granite and valleys of pastures, white sheep and red deer. And to the south, the caves of Torbeg, called the royal caves. They owe their name to Robert Bruce. He had sought refuge there to meditate over fighting his enemy. The invincible courage of a spider desperately weaving his web inspired him and rekindled his willpower. He saw the spider fall and fall again six times over, like a tightrope walker. Seeing this spectacle Robert Bruce made a vow: "I also have undergone six defeats against the English. If the spider succeeds on its seventh try, I will go on the attack again."

The little indefatigable spider of the Isle of Arran succeeded in its seventh try and Robert Bruce set off for war. He defeated King Edward of England and won the battle of Bannockburn singing the martial song "Scots Hey Tuttie Taitie." This was in 1314. And until God called him, he never surrendered to the English. He died in 1329…Six days before John XXII claimed throughout Christianity his recognition as King of Scotland by Avignon (then the Papal Seat). Only one year before, England had renounced the throne of Scotland. Arran claims its part of the glory for the Treaty of Edinburgh. The island faithfully honors the name of Robert Bruce: to squash a spider brings bad luck.

When you sail along Arran on the port side is the long and fine peninsula of Kintyre which inspired Paul McCartney, the Celtic Beatle, to write the song, the sad "Mull of Kintyre." Same beaches, same valleys, same mountains of granite, same rich pastures, same sheep, same deer, same forests as on Arran. A bonus for Philip, his first whiskey stop.

Kintyre has its malt Mecca in Campbeltown a few swimming strokes from Islay (pronounced *eye-luh*). There were thirty distilleries in this village. They were flourishing in the thirties but now only two remain: Spring Bank and Glen Scotia still haunted by its former owner drowned in Campbeltown Lake.

Philip and Tony salute his soul as they go north by the Celtic Cross of Skipness Point which leads into the immense Loch Fyne. After hitting breakers, formed by the opening between the two points, the trawler majestically enters.

Majestically, that's for sure, he smoothly sails by Crarae Gardens before anchoring in Inveraray. The Georgian town in eighteenth century style, looks like a white island in the morning light. The Duke of Argyll reigns over this aristocratic Eden. Twelfth in rank and chief of the Campbell Clan, he holds the title of Mac Cailean mor, in Gaelic this means son of Colin the Great. From his castle, built in 1494, he still reigns over 30,000 hectares (74,131 acres), the Argyll Regiment – one of the 16 elite regiments from the Highlands – and the whiskey of his clan.

It's here, in the high towers of Inveraray Castle that Mary Stuart, Queen of Scotland, came to visit her sister, the Duchess of Argyll, and tasted her first glass of *usigue beatha* (Gaelic for eau-de-

LEFT AND ABOVE

Made up of 15 lochs over 14.5 kilometers (9 miles), the Crinan Canal, opened in 1801, to save fishing boats from going around the Mull of Kintyre. Today, only one day is needed for pleasure boats to get to Loch Fyne from Crinan, the small port opposite Isle of Jura.

TO THE RIGHT

Inveraray Castle, at the bottom Loch Fyne, is the ancestral residence of the Duke of Argyll, Chief of the Campbell Clan.

vie). The whiskey of the Argyll house was already considered in 1563 one of the oldest and one of the most noble Scottish whiskeys.

Down from there, the scenic road where the signposts say "rest and be thankful" takes you to the sheltered port of Lochgilphead. You can buy salmon, kippers and smoked herrings there and taste delicate oysters.

Today's goal is to confront the high seas so as to get to Oban, the "gateway to the isles." A gateway, the Crinan Canal, leads you to it. It opens onto Jura a stoney flatland, a string of islands, and onto Mull in the distance. Crinan is a succession of locks. Philip's boat, *Pêcheur d'Images*, is locked into the little basins. Other boats

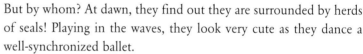

also await the opening of the locks. The locks are manually opened and closed. In the spirit of Scottish fair play, Philip is signaled to go first. It's Tony's job – a great copilot – to adjust the ropes which dock and hoist up the boat.

Suddenly a man jumps up onto the bridge of the boat. Without a word and hardly greeting anyone, he goes about working away on the bridge. After they have gone through two or three locks, the man finally introduces himself as the owner of the next yacht and a doctor at Oban. He helps Philip and Tony all day. The end of Crinan Canal looks like an arm of water that runs into the sea. Going from one basin to another and from one lock to the next, you go down between alignments of boats and forest gardens until the

last stop. At the foot of the passage, built on the side of a cliff, stands a pub attached to the only port hotel. With its decoration of party lights, it answers to the flashing lighthouse facing the Atlantic.

At last, the open sea. There lies Jura, full of wild palm trees. Its waters seem to be inhabited by strange periscopes. There's a feeling of being encircled and spied upon. But by whom? At dawn, they find out they are surrounded by herds of seals! Playing in the waves, they look very cute as they dance a well-synchronized ballet.

The fishermen of the area think less of them. They know that seals eat half of their weight in food, that they multiply like rabbits, that they transmit diseases to fish. Here the little fishing boats still have free fishing without quota, calendar or weight. For the fishermen, seals destroy the fishing banks and are therefore their enemy. Only the Celtic legends stop them from declaring total war against these creatures. The legend attributes magic powers to the seals and honors the *Selkies*, the half seal, half human, mythical generous creatures. But the hard life of the sailors is unfortunately not a legend. Not even a Celtic one. Not even here, in Scotland.

The inhabitants of the Isle of Seil,
to the south of Oban,
are fishermen and farmers.

LEFT

The Isle of Balnahua.
These open slate mines were
worked in the beginning of
the twentieth century.

RIGHT

The lighthouse on the
Isle of Fladda lights Luing
Sound between Jura and Seil.

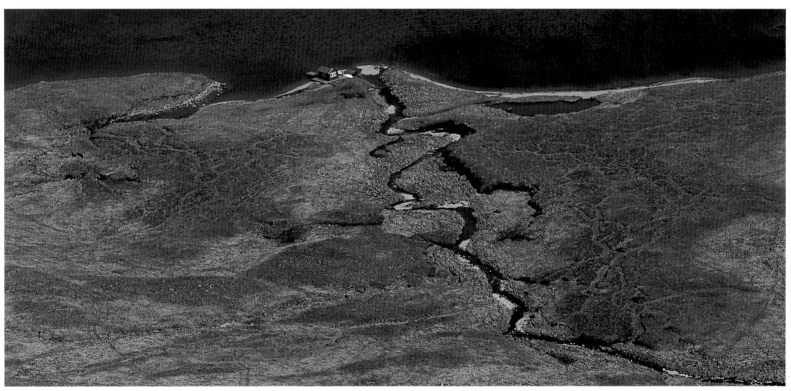

On the coast of the
Isle of Jura, the peat bogs
flow into the sea.

*Anchorage in the early morning,
at Crinan, while waiting for
the first lock to open.*

*The Easdale shuttle off
the west coast of the Isle of Seil.*

ABOVE

Fishermen's cottages around
Crinan Port.

OPPOSITE

The Isle of Gigha, between
Islay and the west side of
Tarbert Loch, a little paradise
bathed by the Gulf Stream.

ABOVE

The Isle of Jura, "the breast of Jura,"
at 785 meters (2,575 feet)
at the foot of Loch An t-Sioh.

LEFT

Between the Mainland and the Isle of Seil,
"the bridge over the Atlantic." In the Scottish humor:
"The only bridge over the Atlantic."

OPPOSITE

The Isle of Islay.
Portnahaven with the Rinns of Islay lighthouse,
automated the 19th of February, 1998.

From Jura to Islay, there is only one long stretch of sea. You go down it only after having slightly touched Scarba where the most violent currents of Scotland are found. Even in a very calm sea, one meter waves can sweep over the water.

Islay is a rich island. Barges loaded with barley unload at Port Ellen. The barley is dried on the spot. The cargo is shared amongst the most iodined distilleries of Scotland. The strongest malts of the island are made here. Marine whiskeys! *Lagavulin* and *Laphroaig* compete over the same river and black peat. The best fragrance of wrack (seaweed) compost, will help the experts decide which whiskey will be the best. They love or hate it…with passion.

On the road to Oban, small ports with white houses and slate roofs can be seen standing against the rocks. Scarba, Toberonochy, Cullipool, Easdale, little islands and islets, and hamlets, make their living from slate. They are called "black isles." Their nickname comes from those big open quarries that form a kind of metallic gray causeway. Boats transport their load to the big ports of the continent. Australia, New Zealand, and even the United States have brought work to the slate workers of the Highlands.

The trawler, *Pêcheur d'Images*, glides to the Isle of Seil attached to the coast by a little stone bridge covered in heather. The bridge is ten meters (32.8 feet) long and has the fairy-like name of the "only bridge across the Atlantic!" A very original but not as ironic name as one would think, as on the other side of this little strait lies the Atlantic! A lunch break takes you to Tigh-an-Truish-Inn, an inn built in the eighteenth century, where meals are served with farm salmon fished that same morn-

ing at the salmon farm at Kilninver.

The region is known for salmon of the Highlands. An old law forbids fishing on Sundays. Know what day it is when you stop to have a gourmet meal! In Scotland, it's always "Sunday is closed."

We are now in Kilbride, its ferry full of laughing children who come and go to school. They call out to Philip and Tony: "A photo, a photo!" On the quay, Philip has just put down his bag full of rolls of film and in five minutes, villagers surround him. "Can we do something for you? Can we help you?"

Immediately, Philip is known. An article in *Classic Boat* describes his photo documentary project about their own Scotland on the sea, the land they love. The article in the newspaper gets around. The local newspaper takes it up. Philip Plisson is the attraction of the day especially since his catch is a good one. Philip admits that he's exhausted, he only sleeps three hours a night, not more… He had started his odyssey at the end of March at the beginning of spring. The trip around Scotland by sea has put a spell on him. The evening light has given him his most beautiful shots. The sunrise, his best awakenings. It's always around eleven o'clock when the sun goes down over the horizon in the sea. Three o'clock when it comes up again, three hours between midnight and dawn, between the two orange yellow halos that surround the range of blues, from azure to navy.

Oban, point of anchorage and crossroads between the Hebrides at the extreme west and the Lochs that lead to both the Great North and the east coast, will help him get his strength back.

Mc Arthurs head lighthouse lights
the entrance to the Sound of Islay, sea arm,
between the Isles of Jura and Islay.

*Peat and fly fishing are a real ode
to nature in Scotland.*

FOR PAGES 38-39

The Firth of Lorn, sea arm,
between the Mainland and
the Isle of Mull.

Oban, protected by the Isle Kerrera,
is a Victorian style fishing port that
developed in the nineteenth century with
the arrival of steamboats and the train.

If style makes the man, Oban owes its Victorian status to a strong forceful woman, Queen Victoria, also known for her austerity. She added this pearl to the west of the Highlands, to the crown, at her Diamond Jubilee. It was in 1897 that the Queen and Empress of India transformed the little fishing port into a fashionable sea resort. Her Majesty, who had rheumatism, drew from Oban's local climate, which is temperate and mild, a kind of avant-garde sea therapy.

The architecture of the town does not reflect, nevertheless, the mark of royalty. No, this port stays a port with a soul of a port. It owes a lot to the knowledgeable inspiration and industrial ambition of the Stevenson Brothers. A century earlier, glass in hand, they had decided to transform the family brewery into a distillery. From then on, Oban's destiny was sealed. The life in Oban swung between a port town and a growing town. Its whiskey, still famous, has acquired a rich and complex texture over time. This single malt is praised by impressed connoisseurs who delight in the smell of seaweed and the sea.

In Oban, there always reigns a strong desire to sail away. The city is a port opening onto the isles – those close to the farthest Hebrides – and on the Caledonian Canal that splits the Highlands from loch to loch up to the North Sea.

Philip boards a trawler docked on the quay. The captain and his men are busy with their nets. Their wooden crates and baskets full of shellfish. The boat's bridge is covered in piles of scampi looking like a crumpled up carpet of coral. Philip, who feels at ease bargaining, names his price at the fish stall. The captain nods, deal done. In just three minutes, Tony cooks up a good soup. This is a

Founded in 1794, the Oban Distillery produces a great malt with a smoked and peated aroma. This gets high marks in all the whiskey bibles.

good excuse to taste before dinner, traditional sea products of Oban with a glass of muscadet! On the quay, one of the fishermen is curious about what they are eating and comes towards Philip and Tony to get a better look.

He asks, "Do you also eat the heads?"

"That's the best part," answers Philip.

"But," says the Scotsman as if he's offended by this faux-pas to local high society etiquette, "you don't eat scampi heads when you have such a beautiful boat!"

On these words, our duo go off to the local oceanographic museum. Including giant rays (so big that they could fit into an electric power plant), there are also giant lobster claws magnified by the thick glass of their rocky tank.

Of course, the first thing to do is to go up McCaig's Folly. McCaig was a half-benefactor half-crazy banker who constructed

his own personal Coliseum in 1897. The architecture is in the same spirit as the visions of grandeur from the Victorian era. The Tower dominates over the furthest coasts and islands. The view from the top of the Tower makes the horizon look even further away and definitely makes you feel like going out to sea. It looks down onto Kerrera, Easdale and Seil. Groups of long-haired sheep can be seen grazing away in the distance. The Isle of Mull stands out in the west and will certainly be on the menu tomorrow.

Tonight, it's time to relax. Marie-Brigitte Plisson, Philip's wife, an energetic and feminine woman, arrives straight from her Trinité-sur-Mer in Brittany. "Bevet Breizh" (Long live Brittany) and "Long Live Scotland!" Together, they decide to go to the local Indian Restaurant, another vestige of the nostalgic Victorians. Neil Corbassan, financial director of oil operations for Elf in the North Sea, traveled across Scotland from his headquarters in Aberdeen, to share with his friends, a cheese nam and chicken tandoori. Their evening ends in the joyful stupor of a typical Irish pub. The girls there are all red-heads, as if they had come out of a casting for a television series or a beer commercial. A drummer inspired by the shanty's story holds his drumsticks like a pencil, beating out the rhythm as he taps on his bodhran (a little drum made of dried sheepskin). The rhythm of shanties and working chants is stressed by alternating solos and choruses. The flute squeaks a little tonight. The

violin calls out plaintively. Beneath the crystalline voice of the singer, you can imagine a future Elaine Morgan or Karen Matheson. You sing with her. In front of her, you drink, next to her you dance and beneath the creamy froth of Guinness, you read into the thoughts of these beauties.

That morning, the quays of Oban are bustling with two

kinds of daily traffic: the fishing squadrons and the ferries. The fish is delivered by the fishermen to the wholesale fish markets and then they get ready to go out to sea again for three weeks. You might also come across crews of Bretons in transit and thanks to an oyster farmer from Douarnenez who has lived in Oban all his life, Philip finds out where they are docked and decides to meet them as soon as he can. Oban is also a maritime crossroads and a main ferry stop. The ferry culture is an integral part of the country's customs. It simplifies the lives of people on the coast. You take it like a bus. Everything runs smoothly on board. You barely park your car and before you know it you're almost there. You have just enough time to go up on the bridge where the smell of fish 'n chips wafts through the air. You can take a ferry to Colonsay, a little islet detached on the port side of the coast or to Jura or Islay in the south. And already you can dream of the misty Hebrides way up beyond Skye.

Oban is dominated by an unfinished circular building: It's called "Mc Caig's Folly" (1897), the idea of a banker who wanted to fight against unemployment. Today an observation area has been installed which gives a panorama of the Sound of Mull.

In the inlets of the isle, natural havens can be found to moor a boat.

*Beautiful anchorage at the foot of the Natural History Centre in Glenmore
on the southern coast of the Ardnamurchan Peninsula.*

To the northeast of Mull, Tobermory, founded by the Duke of Argyll
in the nineteenth century, is a harbor protected by the little island
of Calve. This was the last stop made by Commander Charcot
before he disappeared in the Arctic in 1936.

The necessary ferries of the Caledonian Mac Brayne Company. These are probably the best way to go around the Hebrides Archipelago.

Mull is less than an hour away by ferry from Oban. Philip lays anchor. He goes along its indented coastline swept by countercurrents and whipped by nasty winds. Forty minutes later, he's in front of Torosay Castle. It stands guard at the foot of Duart, a property that has belonged to the MacLean clan since the wars of Independence.

There are only two things that you can do on Mull: Go off on the one lane road that leads to the extreme west to get to the little islet of Iona: it is here in the fourth century that Saint Colomba left Ireland to Christianize Scotland, the other Gaelic country. The sacred grass of Iona shelters Scotland's first Christian cemetery. The view over the rocks, from the ruins of a convent, or from vestiges of an abbey, looks on to Staffa. This jutting peak of granite is a bird reserve. The trawler, *Pêcheur d'Images*, will soon go around it avoiding the dangerous currents around the coast. This adds to the island's natural defenses.

The mountainous Isle of Mull is full of deer which graze all the way down to the edge of the high chalky cliffs. Two clans live there: the MacLeans and the MacDonalds. You find them everywhere. They are fishermen, hunters, and barmen. It's still a great mystery how these names have survived and remained so numerous.

At the time Saint Louis reigned in France, the two clans sharing the isle were very busy staining the land and heather with their blood. With their slashing claymores (the heavy metal polished sword), they hunted each other down and cut one another to pieces.

Peace arrived under the name *Florencia*. Its name could have been Providence. *Florencia* was a great Spanish vessel richly sculptured in gold, a galleon of fifty-two cannons, one of the most beautiful ships of the Invincible Armada. The storm had diverted the ship on the Bay of Tobermory. The lord of the region was none other than Lachlan Mo'or MacLean, known as the "Great Lachlan." The emissary of Don Pareira, the desperate captain of the *Florencia*, came to see him and demanded, "Give us immediately food to feed the 400 soldiers on our ship." The emissary insisted on these words: "They are great soldiers and we have excellent cannons." Not used to being talked to like this, the Great Lachlan answered by calling together the best warriors of his clan. He called a council in the presence of Pareira and because of the bloody reputation of the MacLeans, Pareira wisely spoke in a more humble tone!

However after lots of false promises Pareira finally managed to repair his damaged boat, to take on food, and with a good wind coming up, he could think of going back to Spain before too long. But Lachlan, who was wary of Pareira's unkept promises, had forced him, as acknowledgment of payment, into giving him a contingent of volunteer Spaniards. They would fight with him to help him defeat the MacDonalds once and for all...and as a guarantee, he kept a group of Spanish officers as hostages. He also sent on board the *Florencia* a young man from his family, Donald, a bold and proud mountain chief. His job was to come back with his pockets full of gold.

Impatient, Pareira didn't wait for his officers to be given back. He put up his sails and put Donald in irons. All sails to the wind...

The *Florencia* got ready to leave the Bay of Tobermory when

Saint Colomba's Tomb in the Abbey of the Sacred Isle of Iona, cradle of Scottish Christianity.

Tobermory, a village of the Highlands is without a doubt the most colorful.

RIGHT

Terminus of the little ferry of Ulva to the west of Mull is an important center for shellfish.

a huge explosion filled the sky and the sea. It was the *Florencia*...it sank into the deep waters of Tobermory within minutes. The young Donald with the courage of a Highlander sacrificed his life to the clan; chained in the gallows near the stock of gun powder he lit a wick to the powder.

Since the year 1600, the Isle of Mull has perpetuated the legend of the galleon, its sunken treasure and the story of young Donald who had chosen to die for his clan. To this day his heroic act entertains evenings in Scotland around the fire. Even at the MacDonalds'.

Night has fallen over Tobermory (in Gaelic this means "Mary's well"). The moon grows pale on the low multi-colored houses – golden yellow, blue slate, ochre or grenadine – surrounding the deepwater bay. This is the last image Commandant Charcot saw of the Isle of Mull before disappearing into the Arctic in 1936...

The open sea is only a sheep's leap away from there. Towards Coll on the starboard side then along the Ardnamurchan Peninsula.

The Sound of Mull rumbles under the ruins of the Ardtornish Castle. Rocky banks scattered with white sandy creeks, colonies of guillemots, terns and Torda penguins fight over the cliff tops.

Philip takes photos of the comic wiggling of the puffin-monks. Because of their red, yellow and blue colored beaks, they are called by their exotic name, sea parrots. A million couples have been estimated. 90% inhabit the Hebrides, the lost isle of Saint Kilda at the extreme west and the Shetland Islands. Philip has fun taking pictures of them diving and their spectacular fishing. The crew is amused at the "parrots" funny looking heads as dozens of little fish hang like a silver moustache over their hooked beaks. Philip also take photos of rabbit holes on the cliffs "stolen" by the puffins to make a nest for their only chick.

Ardnamurchan Point is the last promontory on the peninsula. It is crowned with a lighthouse that watches over Coll, Muck, Eigg and Rúm, four large rocks (two of these are inhabited) in the middle of the sea on the way to the big isles. Philip takes a moment to point his camera on the lookout tower. He has had his eye on all the lighthouses of Europe from the farthest Orkneys to Gibraltar. He hopes to capture the memory of these faithful monuments, a fair homage to their keepers...Sometimes they too are nestled on the cliffs, in all seasons and in all kinds of weather. For decades, they have set their revolving luminous hearth to guide ships in dark nights and through fog.

Times are changing, even in Scotland. As everywhere, lighthouses and the beacons of the Northern Lighthouse Board have been forced to automate. The last keepers have been taken off their lighthouse by boat or by helicopter. Philip has seen these men leave, the memory of the sea and the look of survival deep in their eyes.

They humbly take one last look at their concrete masts planted like a sword amidst the rocks. When no one's watching,

making sure that no camera surprises them, they secretly wave good-bye to them, fighting to keep back their tears. It's a good thing that sailors know how much they owe to these hermit saviors. To thank them, public associations have been organized, to preserve these sites and their stories.

Tomorrow, these lighthouses will become museums. On Ardnamurchan, they will relate the legend of the sea…The lights, the storms, the fog, the night watches, the rescues…

A natural wildlife museum of moors and rocks, in the wind facing the ocean.

Mallaig, fishing harbor and last stop at the end of the peninsula, has been a historical place, since 1746. Bonnie Prince Charlie, the last Stuart, the legitimate pretender to the throne of Scotland, England and Ireland, made it his refuge. Today, the railroad that comes from Glasgow stops there. At the other side of the station, yet another a ferry invites people for the short crossing to Port Armadale…On the way to Skye, the winged isle, the loved isle.

On the Caledonian Mac Brayne ferries,
the trip to the Hebrides is like being on a cruise ship.

FOR PAGES 54-55

Sky over the Ardnamurchan Peninsula.

The Isle of Staffa.

The octagonal regularity of the basaltic columns is such that it seems sometimes difficult to realize that it's a natural phenomena.

Here is also the same volcanic phenomena as the Giant's Causeway in Ulster (Northern Ireland). It is after having visited Fingal's Caves that Mendelssohn wrote the "Hebrides Overture" in 1829.

The Isle of Skye, along Dunvegan.

Green mountains, gray rocks and torrents. Skye is also full of purple moors and thistle, heather and black peat. It shelters Celtic memories and memories of legitimist Scotland. It has done so since 1746, when the dawn of history revealed the clans of the faithful. Skye was the last stop before exile or death.

A year before, commanded by the Irishman Walsh, the *Du Teillay*, a frigate of sixteen cannons, left from Roscoff in the north of Brittany. It had embarked a slight, blond, 25-year-old mysterious passenger. It was Prince Charles Edward Stuart. He was the grandson of James II of England, the Catholic King defeated in Ireland on the Boyne, by William of Orange.

Bonnie Prince Charlie had grown up in France, his second country. After 18 days on the sea and a brief victory against the English at Cape Lizard, he set foot on the banks of Loch nan Uamh on the Ardnamurchan Peninsula near Mallaig. Philip Plisson is here also on his fisherman's quest for images.

Bonnie Prince Charlie felt lonely, very lonely. His clans dreamt of seeing him at the head of one of Louis XV's fleets. The King of France was their ally, *Auld Alliance*, obliged. His clans were not only waiting desperately for the Prince to arrive, but also for soldiers, money and arms. The chief of the Cameron clan preoccupied by dark premonitions he had had, advised Charles to put off the war of liberation for a few months. Charles refused. Scotland was his kingdom. He was King "*de jure*." He would never back down. He would take back the throne for the Stuarts.

The rest is called Culloden…Glorious name, damned name, the field of honor and funeral march. On the moors of Inverness, the battle was fought against five thousand brave Highlanders draped in plaid, of brightly colored tartans, armed with heavy claymores. Fighting them was the English cavalry of the Duke of Cumberland: 9000 men, well-trained and well-equipped. The white rosette of the Jacobites (from the Latin *jacobus* – partisans of James II – the Prince was his grandson), fell under the bayonets, and lances of the red tunics: "If I draw back, kill me," commanded Bonnie Prince Charlie. His officers were surrounded and burnt alive in Old Leanach's farm. The survivors swore to protect their leader.

Scotland lost a battle…Didn't it lose the war? Alas, yes! The retreat towards the west coast through burning villages was dramatic. They landed between Arisaig and Mallaig. A French boat, armed by Louis XV, brought money and arms. It embarked some refugees, took them to Corrodale and Benbecula in the outer Hebrides, before sailing back to Brittany…The flag at half-mast.

Bonnie Prince Charlie finally arrived on Skye. He was disguised as a maid and called himself Betty Burke. On this island where Gaelic refuses to give an inch to the English language and where bagpipes are called *piobaidreachd* and whiskey *uisgue beatha*, Charles' followers felt out of reach at last. Throughout the Highlands, Cumberland tracked the doomed Jacobites, easily spotted because they made the sign of the cross and raised their glass over water. This simple gesture was quickly deciphered. It was a secret toast to their King gone over the sea…To drink to the health of their sovereign, led to the gallows.

OPPOSITE

Neist Point, on the west of Skye, where the houses of the three families of the lighthouse keepers have been made into bed and breakfasts.

Throughout the Highlands, prisoners were led in their rags to jail. The luckiest were dumped in the holds of ships and sent to the New World or the Austral Seas.

Even on Skye, Bonnie Prince Charlie was in danger. The 20th of June, two months after Culloden, in an isolated inn in Portree, he said goodbye to the beautiful, 23-year-old Flora Mac-Donald, the heroine of the Jacobites. He was two years older than she but he had lost more than one life in battle! In his red and black kilt and a plaid thrown over his shoulders, he bowed and swore to her that he would see her again, in Saint James' Palace. But this was not to be. Flora was chained in the Tower of London.

Bonnie Prince Charlie headed towards France with no arms for survival left, except for a bottle of whiskey and a bottle of cognac. He attached them to his belt and embarked for the little island of Raasay. There he was given shelter in a forest hut. After having climbed mountains, gone around the basalt peak of Old Man of Store and come down the cliffs, he took shelter in a cave. His flight lasted eight days. At last, a French boat – *L'Heureux* (in French it means "the joyful one") – so inappropriately named – pulled him up on board. It was the 20th of September, 1746. He would never see Scotland again or Flora MacDonald or the High-landers wearing the white rosette. He left the mountains and the green valleys, the heather and the red sky of Skye to become him-self a lost cause. His heart cried for Culloden and Flora. She was his Juliet and he her Romeo. Their Celtic legend is inspired by their shattered destiny. It still hovers over Skye.

An island ballad remains: *The Skye Boat Song*:
Speed Bonnie Boat
Like a bird on the wing
Onward the sailors cry
Carry the lad
That is born to be king
Over the sea to Skye! Skye!

All of Skye Island is a legend. On a visit to Dunvegan Castle, on the edge of the loch, on the west coast, where the MacLeod's residence has stood for the last 700 years, the story of the Fairy Flag is told. It's like a legend should be. It's about a magic flag given by a fairy to the fourth leader of the clan so as to make him invisible.

The writer Kenneth White tells us the story of the MacDonalds and MacLeods fighting over the ownership of the island. The two clans set off to sea at the same time and raced towards the future "homeland of the Gaëls." Their boats were bow to bow only a few strokes away from the isle. Suddenly, one of the MacDonalds cut off his hand and threw it onto the beach (as though he were planting a sword or a flag!) thus claiming Skye for his clan.

Recognizing a MacLeod from a MacDonald, a MacLean from a MacQueen or from a MacMillan, is easy on the islands. The wearing of the kilt which symbolizes resistance and unsubmissiveness was forbidden by the English in 1747, by the "Act of Abolition and Proscription of the Costume of Highlands." Today, it is still elegantly worn at official dinners. Tartan with big red squares, signifies a MacLean, green black and yellow a MacNeil, yellow and black a MacLeod...

On that day, the peninsula of Trotternish, in the north, fief of the MacDonalds in their little green blue red checkered tartan, offers its untamed beauty. The Kilt Rock Waterfalls rush down directly from a high steep cliff into the sea. Traditional thatched roof houses can be seen here and there on the cliffs. This view makes you hungry. Marie-Brigitte Plisson, a great copilot and connoisseur of gastronomy, looks for the best restaurant in her guide book.

Where does one dine? The Three Chimneys where they serve original and creative cuisine? From the book she reads aloud, "One of the best restaurants in Scotland, reservations necessary." So off we go. Goodbye Dunvegan. We stop on the way and she reserves for four. When Philip and his little clan arrive, the parking lot is full of cars and not just any cars: two Jaguars, a Rolls, a Bentley...The address is obviously well known!

This is where they experience their first ode to haggis.

The haggis is a Scottish national dish. It's a traditional dish. Burn's supper is the annual dinner given to honor the poet Robert Burns (1759-1796), who wrote *Scotland, Women and Whiskey*. Scotland alone has erected more statues for Burns than the whole world has for Shakespeare. The haggis is a stuffing made from sheep minced giblets, barley and onions. It's served with turnip purée and a single malt golden whiskey. On Skye, there's only one *Talisker* (a strong whiskey) that goes great with haggis.

It's a tradition to begin the meal by playing the bagpipes. The maitre d', also dressed in a kilt, presents the dish like a holy object. He delicately puts it on the table, unsheathes his dirk (a dagger) and in a sharp accent sings his sacred ode playing on intonations and strong rhythms:

> Fair fa' your honest, sonsie face,
> Great Chieftain o' the Pudding-race!
> Aboon them a' ye tak your place,
> Painch, tripe, or thairm:
> Weel are ye wordy o' a grace
> As lang's my arm.
> The groaning trencher then ye fill,

OPPOSITE PAGE TO THE LEFT:

*Masts are put up here
to dry nets after fishing.*

RIGHT

*Little dinghies of the west coast
often take risks by anchoring
or collecting their lobster traps.*

Your burdies like a distant hill,
Your pin wad help to mend a mill in time
'o need,
While thro' your pores the dews distil like
amber bead.

His knife see rustic Labour dight,
An' cut ye up wi' ready slight,
Trenching your gushing entrails bright,
like onie ditch;
And then, O what a glorious sight, warm-
reekin, rich!

Ye Pow'rs what mak mankind your care
And dish them out their bill o' fare,
Auld Scotland wants nae skinking ware
That jaups in luggies;
But if ye wish her gratefu' prayer,
Gie her a Haggis!

The Maitre d' energetically sinks his dagger into the still burning stuffed dish then proceeds to slice up the rest. Glass of *Talisker* whiskey in hand, the assembly answers him with a vibrant *Slainté* (cheers) and it's time to eat!

*At the foot of Mount Alasdair, Loch na Cuilce extends
into a fresh water lake, Loch Coruisk. It's probably
the most beautiful anchorage in the Isle of Skye.*

In the west of Skye, the cliffs plunge over 300 meters (984 feet) into the sea.

Eileandonan Castle is the coming together of three lochs
leading to the Isle of Skye from the mainland.
Restored in the beginning of the twentieth century,
it was built in the thirteenth century to protect the Kings of Scotland.

The approach to the island from the sea.
Here is the entrance to Loch na Cuilce at the foot of the Cullins.

FOR PAGES 66-67
The Cullins are a mountain range reaching 900 meters (2,952 feet)
dominated by the peak of Sgarr Alasdair (993 meters – 3,061 feet).

FOR PAGES 68-69

Aerial view of the mountain range forming the south of Lewis Island,
the largest island of the Outer Hebrides.

The southeast is the most arid part of Harris Island.
It is formed by a multitude of lochs sheltering small fishing boats.

What a contrast between the east (LEFT)
and the west of Harris Island. (RIGHT)

FOR PAGES 74-75

Seilebost beach, on the west of Harris, is preserved for tourists.

The site of Callanish Standing Stones go back to the Stone Age
at the beginning of the Bronze Age (3,000 – 1,500 BC).
Sun and death were worshiped here.

BELOW

An old shepherd's hut in the center of Lewis Island.

On North Uist, the sea and the lowlands permanently mingle.

LEFT

The southern interior road of Harris reveals
a grandiose mineral world.

Black faced sheep give the famous wool
to make Harris tweed.

Thatched roofs are the traditional habitat
of the fishermen in North Uist.

Between Benbecula and North Uist, kilometers
of beaches spread out and are separated in low tide
by the emerald rias.

The deep lochs of the Outer Hebrides are particularly
adapted shelters for the reproduction of Scottish salmon.

LEFT

A beach at South Uist.

ABOVE AND RIGHT

On Lewis Island, the production of peat is an important source of income as is traditional fishing off Stornoway, capital of the Outer Hebrides.

The Atlantic Ocean, to the west of
the Hebrides, is a rich fishing zone.
Boats from Lorient come together
to ship the spectacular take every week.

The cargo ship Pétrel, transports at night,
through Loch Shell, in the south
of Stornoway, the already weighed catch
of its five 55 meter long fishing boats.

On the other hand, the Jego Quéré cargo
has signed agreements with the Scottish
fish market in Lochinver, in the north
of Ullapool. Here trawlers unload their huge
catch. A shuttle is set up every week
to get to Lorient in 24 hours.

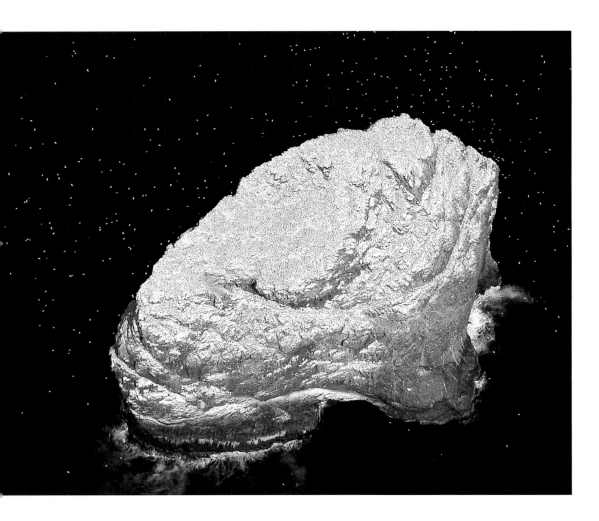

Saint-Kilda is the most spectacular of the archipelagos situated off the shores of Great Britain.
It's in Hirta, the main island of the group, that the largest gathering of petrels in Great Britain are found
on its highest cliffs. On the neighboring isle of Boreray and its two rocks,
the largest colony of gannets in the world lives.

The isle of North Uist mingles stretches of land and sea.
This gives a good salty taste to the sheep.

Lewis Island. The legend goes that the menhirs, in the form of a cross,
on the site of Callanish, were an astronomical observation point...

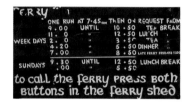

Southeast of Harris Island spread out the most beautiful sandy beaches where big waves from the Atlantic roll in.

The isles in the west are a world beyond the world. Skye is just a handful of hours away from these eroded mountains that bar the horizon. They protect the continent and the Highlands from any imaginary arctic invasion.

Here, also, Bonnie Prince Charlie bore his cross. South Uist, with its vast virgin plains is inhabited by sheep with thick wool and black heads. Apparently, the sail of the desperate wandering Prince touched Barra and the rocks at the extreme south. In his travel log, Philip scrupulously notes the string of Gaelic names for his next stops, they will be his last treasures from the sea. Cille Bharra – and its convent built on the cliffs – Rhudha na h-Ordaig, Loch Druidibeg, Bagh nam Faoileann, Ceann A Deas na Hearadh, Uibist A'Tuath, these are like barricades to stop the English language from stepping in. These names spread out all along the sculptured coasts whipped by the east winds and are bordered by a chain of blue and naked mountains covered in thin heather.

The sea fills up the horizon. It cleans the land, bathes the capes, floods into the grottos, and whips the rocks. Uist is striped with Venetian-like Canals. It looks like a labyrinth in the sea. It takes longer to pass from South Uist to North Uist by road, via the Isthmus of Benbecula than to cross Little Minch by ferry, a turbulent stretch of sea which opens on to the Hebrides and then Skye.

The canals go from twenty meters long (65.6 feet), to fifty (164 feet) or a hundred (328 feet)....The ferries are all sizes. They sail the seas in every direction in gusts of wind and heavy currents. They dance to the music of a nautical ballet.

They leave from Oban, about eight hours from Uist or from Ullapool on Loch Broom in the north of the Highlands, twice around the clock from there. They sail past the Southern Islands, they dock in the center on Harris, Tarbert and stop for awhile at Stornoway, the port of Leogach, the isle of peat popularly baptized "Lewis" by the English.

They let out passengers, soaked with freezing sea spray, full of warm beer and the smell of cold tobacco. Their heads full of images from the world of shadow and light created by Robert Louis Stephenson, the wandering engineer who illuminated his century. He had gone from the lighthouses and fog of the Great North to the fevers of the South Seas and the Gold Rush in California...The passengers have that romantic look in their eyes as did Walter Scott, who embarked in 1814 aboard a ship belonging to The Northern Lighthouse Company. The writer brought back from his trip, his book, *The Lord of the Isles*, an ode honoring these sentinels, the lighthouses in the extreme west.

On these islands like a frieze in the horizon, you can walk around the Standing Stones of Callanish. Man had put up a solar circle in homage to his gods there, four thousand years ago. They are

still standing today and the Druidic perfume of the past merges with the Christian incense of today.

Our passengers who have come here off the ferryboat, read and reread Kenneth White. They all identify themselves to Brendan, the hero of "Atlantica."

"He had the isles in his head
He was born amidst the isles
He had grown up amongst the isles
He knew the Hebrides by heart
For him the world nothing but isles
And the sky also."

Suddenly, Philip also becomes Brendan. His heart goes out to Saint Kilda, "insular microcosm and utopic land." For a thousand years it had lived in perfect autarky until the forced evacuation of its rare inhabitants in 1930, they were only 37! The archipelago is 100 kilometers (62.13 miles) from the Hebrides and 200 (124.27 miles) from Oban…Benbecula is on the way there. The small town separates the two Uists (North and South). This is a key landing point. The Cessnas, Pipers, and all the fleet of small tourist planes, land at the air club here as it's the first air strip in the North Atlantic.

Philip prefers the helicopter. How else can you land on the grasslands of Saint Kilda! The black helicopter, an Agusta 109, takes off vertically. Everywhere below you can see the sea, even more sea

and nothing but the sea. It's everywhere. Everywhere!

Soon, above the frothy waves, a grayish shadowy alignment can be seen. They look impatient to be discovered: Boreray, Hirta, Stac an Armin and Stac Lee, a tooth-like rock sticking out of the ocean. Lots of forgotten little islets emerge in a halo of mist from the heat.

The helicopter lands at the foot of the little church of Hirta. It reflects the social life of the local community under the iron hand and the rigorous stern preaching of pastors. The daily service was compulsory. There were three on Sundays. No absence was tolerated.

Here is what is left of Main Street. A little street bordered by low thatched houses built from large stones. They stand along 300 meters (984.2 feet) of bare granite…

Life went on there, for a whole millennium!…Until the very end. Men wearing big beards, vests made of homemade tweed and woolen bonnets with pompoms, held a daily council. They shared the tasks, the most humble tasks. They fished, they hunted, they captured sea birds. This was their art of survival. Its inhabitants shared everything equally. The highest cliffs were like fortifications, the tiniest hole in the rock was a niche, a refuge. For a thousand years, therefore, the forgotten Isle of Saint Kilda, snuggling up in the loneliness of the fog and the night, had only the sea birds as its companions and they were hunted for food, for their feathers and for their oil.

Four calves and ten cows were still left on the island, the 27th of August, 1930. That morning, the *Dunara Castle*, which came over from the continent, embarked the skinny herd. Already, some hundred sheep had produced its effect on the market at Oban. Others refused the call of the shepherds and threw themselves from the cliffs…

At last came the turn for the men to leave. Their names were

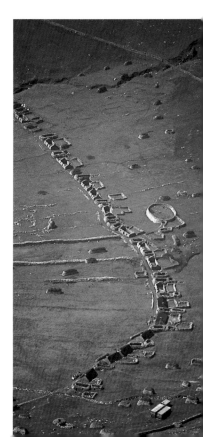

Gillies, Ferguson, MacDonald, Mackinnon…A handful of surnames for the same handful of inhabitants! They left carrying old tattered bags, pulling along crying kids. The women dressed in black blouses and scarves on their oval faces, their hair divided in the middle of their heads, looked like widows out of nowhere. These deeply rooted sea people, became from that moment on, nomads. Against their wishes, the British administration scattered them all over the Duke of Argylle's land. This caused a public uproar of compassion in the beginning but only lasted a short time, then the big book of forgetfulness closed its pages on the memory of the clan.

Today St. Kilda is empty. The army has planted its flag and the geologists their tents. The authorities refuse any kind of settlement on the archipelago. Philip hands over the last postal bag of Royal Mail from the continent to the handful of soldiers that keep guard there under the stars.

A plaque put down in 1987 is all that is left…Forty people accompanied the UNESCO team to St. Kilda to name the site a "Patrimony of the Humanity." They all sang nostalgically "I to the hills will lift mine eyes." Along with this official requiem, the ruins of St. Kilda join the Temples of Egypt, The Taj Mahal, and the Buddhist Pyramid of Borobudur…

In its archives, Edinburgh has the written traces of this tribal micro society, etchings and photos. You can see the men taming its rocks and peaks, the women with fixed smiles on their faces, weav-ing at the wheel. They would try to sell some meters of tweed or some bird's feathers to the rare tourist who would land at Village Bay.

One last photo of the "Celtic reserve." The black helicopter takes off. At 14,000 French Francs an hour, you have to know when to go back to port!

Away from South Uist and Barra, where priests still wear

frocks, Harris and Lewis Islands live the Presbyterian faith. Faith is law. Puritanism obliges: Here you know everything about your neighbor. The pastors in white collars don't hesitate to denounce sinners during their services.

Life here is austere and slow. One wakes up early to do ones chores, to share a broth or a *partan bree* (a soup made of crab), some pink shrimps, mussels from the rocks, and a poor porridge made of oat flour. Lunch comes as an interlude. Dinner is early, at 5:30 when the white sun declines over the horizon. Same menu, same punishment. Haddock is grilled, salted, peppered and dipped in milk to give a little sea flavor to their bland meals.

You finally reach the pub, the unavoidable center of social life there. It's difficult to brighten up an ordinary day here with music. On the islands, a shepherd's pipe is sometimes played, it's a simple bagpipe with no air pouch. On the other hand, the noble violin is always played. Its bow slides or cries depending on what time of the day it is or who is playing it!

Friday is always a big night. The men take out their kilts from their wardrobe, the women their make-up kits.

They are as beautiful as the women of Aberdeen, Inverness or Edinburgh. Friends meet in the pubs or invite one another home,

even satellite television hasn't killed social life here.

Sunday is a different thing. Sunday in the Hebrides is "strictly prohibited – closed."

For the pastors, the day of the Lord belongs to the Lord and to Him alone. You can't take a slice of his life away from Him!

This particular Sunday, Philip and his family are on Harris, isle of mountains and rocks. It's divided into two: lunar scenery with black lakes, and blue sea with low skies and herds of sheep on the moors and heather. First thing in the morning, the landlord tells Philip:

"Today, no room service. It's Sunday..."

"What time do you serve lunch?"

"There's no lunch on Sunday."

"Brunch, maybe?"

"There's no brunch on Sunday."

"And the pub?"

"There's no pub on Sunday."

She ties her scarf and puts her hand on the pocket Bible.

"Excuse me, I'm going to be late for Sunday service."

Tony and Philip decide to "kill Sunday" by improvising a day of fishing. But as soon as Philip takes his fishing rod out of the rented pick-up van, a gray skinned ageless man comes up to him and solemnly says: "Sir, even the shrimp have the right to rest on Sunday."

Golf is the only thing left. At least this is a specific Scottish sport, relaxing, played on private ground, away from indiscrete eyes. There's only one problem for that...they need gas to get there. Again...

"Sorry, the service station is closed...it's Sunday."

A gas station attendant feels sorry for them and serves 20 liters to the charming visitors!

The portrait of the micro society curled up around the Bible and its beer (secretly drunk at home) and its Sundays do not reveal everything about the Hebrides.

The oil of the North Sea, the skillful negotiation by the Norwegians with the Common Market, contributes to the development of Stornoway, the last stitch of Victorian tartan in the islands. Stornoway, is the capital of Lewis, its red facades and its beautiful buildings make it a beautiful happy port. It's is only a stretch of sea away from Ullapool, the biggest of small ports in the Highlands. Many Breton fishermen come there, as a matter of fact lots of Breton trawlers make it their anchor point. Sometimes their boats are 50 to 60 meters (196.8 feet) long and they go out to sea for three weeks. They sail around the whole coast and go from Cape Wrath, around the Northwestern Coast of Scotland and up to Oban, via Lochinver. The Old Man of Stoer (a needle like rock) planted in the sea, stands like an obelisk saluting their passage.

Every Monday, a big Breton trawler, the *Pétrel* leaves Orient. Its cargo is unloaded at the mouth of Loch Shell (or Loch Sealy) on Lewis. The fish is prepared and put into boxes and loaded on trucks going from Plymouth and Roscoff. In all, it takes them three days to get to Brittany and back...the Scottish Sea and Mor Bihan. The Celtic Seas are nourishing seas.

In the Outer Hebrides,
you don't play around
with the rules of life dictated
by the Presbyterian Church.
No activity is tolerated
on Sunday.

ABOVE

Here, the sea is not forgiving.

BELOW

*Eastern Tarbert Loch, between Lewis and Harris,
is a bay sheltered from dominant winds.*

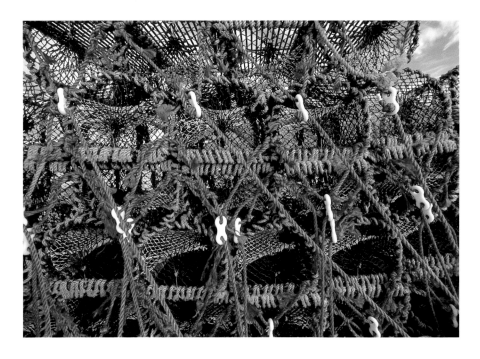

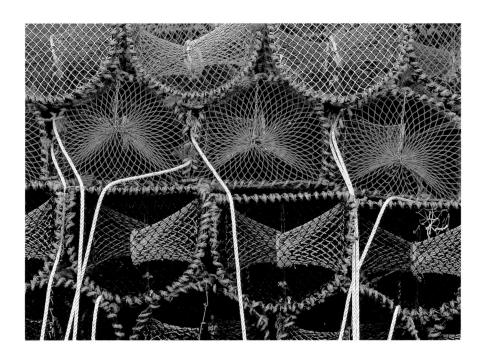

The specialty of the Hebrides is shellfish fishing: crabs, lobsters…Crayfish are so beautiful and appreciated that they are individually stocked and transported in water tanks. The main part of this catch is for the French market and restaurants.

Back to the Mainland by Ullapool, a fishing port especially well sheltered in Loch Broom. This eighteenth century village has also become an appreciated destiny for pleasure boats that sail around the Hebrides.

Linnhe Loch, with the Isle of Mull in the background, is the first stretch of sea that goes
into Fort William, at the south entrance of the Caledonian Canal.

Anchorage in the early morning on the south of Loch Ness.

eturn to Oban.

The ferries of the "Caledonian MacBrayne" company let off the passengers – resident Islanders or Islanders of a day – at the railway pier. Philip and his crew await their turn to dock next to the sailboats already docked. The crew prepares for their new adventure.

They won't be going on the sea for a while. Philip and his crew will be sailing down the Caledonian Canal along the interwoven inland waterway. From Oban to Inverness and from the Hebrides Sea to the North Sea, this profound passageway separates the Highlands into two forests along the banks. The Romans called Scotland Caledonia, "the mounts of great forests." Cliffs all along are still covered in resinous trees.

Sailing out of Oban and into the mouth of Loch Linnhe, the cries of the guillemots and flapping wings of laughing seagulls is enough to distract any young inexperienced skipper trying to deal with choppy seas, bad winds and countercurrents around the isles.

Beyond Fort Williams lie the dormant waters of Great Glen the big valley. Here begins a continuous stretch of water: The black deep waters of the lochs. These natural lakes have been reunited by artificial navigable roads. 180 kilometers (111.85 miles) that divide the Highlands into two. So, the Caledonian Canal goes from Loch Linnhe (last stretch of the Atlantic), and up to the mouth of Moray on the east coast. This Pharaonic construction joining the two seas is a symbol of nineteenth century grandeur.

Its name perpetuates Roman Caledonia. The vestiges of Hadrian's Wall, built from one bank to the other of the Lowlands by the Emperor, are a reminder of an unfinished conquest. It still marks the frontier between Scotland and England. Beyond, stood the bold clans, Picts, Scots and Gaels, faced the enemy legions.

The Caledonian shield is a wonder. It ends at the foot of Spey Valley, on the crest of the Cairngorms, a mountain chain which are an extension of the Grampian Mountains. Its plateaus are covered in wild forests and Arctic flora and Fauna. You might come across the only reindeer herd left in the Great North and any other polar regions.

All is revealed from the wooded slopes of Ben Nevis, the highest peak in Scotland. It is a four hour trek, though a landscape of heather, to the summit which reaches 1344 meters (4409 feet) high. From the top a wonderful view of Gaelic isles crowds the horizon and dominates the Hebrides.

There's skiing in the winter and trekking in the summer. You can eat at the exotic Everest Indian Inn, a chalet with Indian food. Under the snowcapped summit or the eroded slopes, the mountain sparkles like crystal and shines like enamel. It seems as if the valleys

ABOVE

It is well known that when a legend becomes more real than reality, the legend is written... Where are we at with Nessie? Numerous search missions have left from the foot of Urquhart Castle. The monster is still a curiosity.

The banks of the lochs were covered with resinous trees in the last quarter of the century. This corresponded to the demands of the paper industry. Today, these forests have thrown out the fauna and reduced the flora over thousands of acres.

encircling Fort William are spotted with blood. Poetic geologists call these grenadine spots, "little rubies." They give the summits of Scotland a touch of Burmese wealth. Highlanders nostalgically call these nuggets of rocks, the "blood of the brave." It's understandable: Glencoe is only a few pine forests away. In 1692, four years after the deposition of the Catholic King, James II, the soldiers of the Campbell clan – already rallied to William III of England – assassinated the MacDonalds by surprise. The MacDonalds had given them shelter for ten days but had hesitated to swear the same oath of allegiance as the Campbells. They had remained loyal to James II. To the Jacobites.

Their descendants still see the stigma of the massacre in the red rock nuggets. In the winter, the snow buries these dark memories while the skiers in Glencoe descend the slopes uncovering the ghosts of the assailants unsheathing their claymores.

Fort William also evokes the memory of battle. An English general, Monk, was at the head. This man preferred the banner to the cross. As early as 1655, he built an impregnable fort in the woods for his red tunics. His strategy was to bar the route to the isles from the Highlanders wearing multicolored tartans.

The ancient garrison city is still colorful today. But now, the colors come from the marks on the thousands of sheep put on the market (the second largest in Scotland) in Fort Williams every week. The largest market is at Lairg, way up north, in Sutherland, where the army evacuated three thousand families in the 1800s replacing them with hundreds of thousands of sheep.

Despite themselves, these new invaders have been a disaster for the Highlands. During The Clearances (forced ethnic evacuations), the farmers that were left, half a century after the defeat at Culloden, were condemned to ruin and exile. Whole villages, destroyed

hamlets, *crofts* of chalk and thatch roofs resembling those in the Hebrides and in the ruins of St. Kilda, were wiped off geological survey maps, thus off the face of the earth…

Today, the sheep are brought in by the truckful, their wool painted blue, red or green.

They are packed in frightened herds in covered markets where the bidding is held. White or black-heads, with fine cottony wool (long and curly or short), rams, sheep and ewes parade in front of a blasé and rustic assembly…For 5 million Scots, there are 50 million sheep! There, under their tweed caps and stiff in their waterproof Barbour, buyers scrutinize their neighbor who has already figured out the condition of the animal, where it had grazed, and what return they would get on their investment. The look on their faces gives them away. They have the quick reflexes of a horse trader buying in a foreign currency. As you might guess, deals are closed in the pub.

Of course, Neptune was chosen to watch over the Caledonian Canal, the Caledonia of the Romans. *Neptune's Staircase*, a series of lochs north of Fort William, links the two seas. One of these lochs is the mythical Loch Ness which has fascinated researchers for the last 1400 years!

Going up the River Lochy and through the succession of lochs makes one claustrophobic. The "art of locks" requires a lot of

patience. You have to wait for hours in the basin, which often receives many boats at the same time. The etiquette is as well-defined

as in golf. In short, it's a time for pastoral philosophizing all the way up to Fort Augustus.

It takes so long to go through the 29 locks that you even have time to walk around the ancient English fort constructed in the beginning of the eighteenth century to look out for any Jacobite rebellion.

Everything here is dedicated to Nessie and the tourist office encourages people to go on cruises with sonar equipment…just in case, the monster, said to be as old as the loch itself, decides to show its face.

The first appearance of the monster is dated 565 AD and signed Saint Colomba. The saint from Ireland set foot on the island of St. Iona and founded a monastery on the banks of this deep lake which in some places is as deep as the North Sea. The legend goes that he himself saw the plesiosaurus.

According to the Benedictines of the Abbey, other texts date from the eighth century. It wasn't until 1933 that the saga started up again. Witnessing, counterwitnessing, photos, staging, amateur films, hoaxes and finally usage of ultra sophisticated technology have filled the files of the "Loch Ness Phenomena Investigation."

The waters in this 39 kilometers (24.23 miles) long giant lake are as black as Guinness. It's estimated that there are 13 million wild salmon…Some of the biggest names in science, including Commandant Cousteau, have given their time and knowledge to

LEFT

At Fort Augustus, close to the Benedictine Abbey, the series of locks of the Caledonian Canal leads to the entrance to Loch Ness 30 meters (98 feet) below.

ABOVE

Castle Stalker on the loch, between Oban and Fort William.

RIGHT

The bank south of Loch Lochy on the Caledonian Canal.

the legend. Nothing. Nobody, not even an underwater robot raking the loch down to the slightest crack could find the uncatchable Nessie whose close cousin is said to inhabit Loch Morar, not far from Skye…

Philip, plunged into the abyss of Jurassic thought, watches the water carefully, when suddenly, ripples form on its surface. He has his camera around his neck ready to capture the inaccessible. Will he succeed? Here where in 1934, Colonel Wilson took a "real" photo that convinced the world for fifty years? Here where Lachlan Stuart, in 1951, mistook three bails of hay under the water for the humps of the dragon? Here, where in 1955, a certain Mac-Nab swore that he had surprised a marine creature as big as the Urquhart Castle? Here, where in 1960, Tim Dinsdale filmed a long oval and dark shape that he described as the "extraordinary humps of a gigantic creature."

The suspense is unbearable. But, not for long…In the shape of a giant reptile, a huge tree trunk suddenly appears on the surface of the water then immediately disappears again…Robert Craig's thesis comes to mind. This Scottish engineer, who kept his feet on the ground, made a good case. Like Loch Morar, Loch Ness is surrounded by very old pine forests. Wooded Heights…Caledonia again. Their fallen trunks live in the depths of the opaque lake. Despite the water pressure, they don't split into pieces. Their composition – resin and gas – preserves them. Sometimes, due to the deterioration of the wood, there is a gas leakage and small bursts of gas cause the trunks to rise to the surface. Once all the gas has escaped and the trunk becomes heavier than the water – it sinks back to the depths of the Loch.

Twenty-four hours a day, image hunters awaiting a worldwide scoop, relay one another to survey the Lock Ness through their binoculars. Without knowing it, without wanting to, and especially without believing it, they tirelessly watch out for floating pine trunks as big as their dreams.

Pêcheur d'Images sails the loch at six or seven knots on average. Adding to the mysteries of the depths, his boat's wake soon ripples out endlessly as if it was blown out by an interior breath. Onboard, imagination increases…

The fog falls over the promontory that dominates Urquhart Castle, enveloping its square towers, drowning its fortifications and putting a veil over the landscape like a soft halo. Philip puts his camera away. He won't pretend to be a paparazzi. Nessie can stay underwater.

Anchorage at the loch north of Loch Oich. Cruises are organized on old barges luxuriously furnished.

At the foot of beautiful properties on the north of Loch Ness are little shelters for dinghies.

Sheep are regularly gathered in the Highlands
for shearing and branding.

The passing place is a culture that is a respect to others.
A cordial wave is made when two cars pass one another.

LEFT

Sheep, the unloved, since the doomed Clearances in the nineteenth century are omnipresent today in the Highland landscape. It is also the primary income of the country.

RIGHT

Weekly market for sheep in Fort William and the largest of the Highlands.

FOR PAGES 116-117

The banks of the lochs are metamorphosed when autumn colors appear at the end of November.

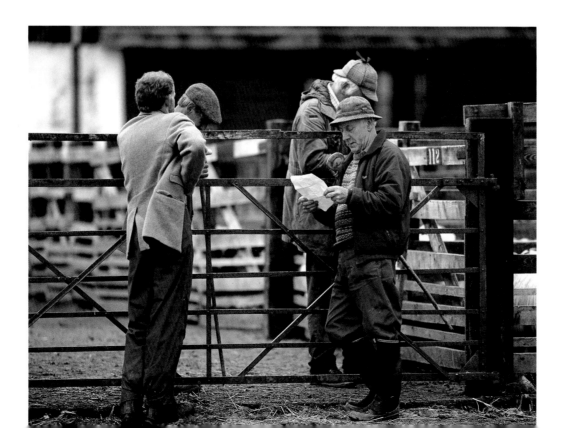

I Inverness looks out on Moray Firth and therefore out to sea. This is not only the coquettish and rustic capital of the Highlands. Here, Flora MacDonald (heroine of the Highlanders) is sculptured in stone and engraved in every heart; the black lands of Culloden, stained with the blood of the Jacobites and the shadows of Shakespeare's ghosts and the tragic reign of Macbeth, remain the sovereign memories of Scotland.

In summer, the city is overpopulated. Holiday goers have transformed the River Ness into a port. Because of its many locks, it is now too narrow for the monster. Many sailboats, lots of which come from Norway, berth here over the winter. *Pêcheur d'Images* also docks for the season in this happy marina where sea gulls dance the day away.

Like Oban in the west, Inverness is the crossroads of the east. It looks on to the valley of Spey, the whiskey road, which is a delight for tourists with its many stops over a triangle of 110 kilometers (68.35 miles). There are many: *Glenlivet, Cardhu, Aberlour, Glenfiddich, Knockandhu, Strathisla,* and *Cragganmore.* You can drive this road like you would sail between beacons…

Peterhead, on the slopes, is just above

Aberdeen. This port town supplies all the fish for the Northern Europe market. Even the French markets receive shellfish, seafood, mauve sea urchins – every kind of seafood – and whitefish… it all comes from Peterhead. There's enough here for the whole of Scotland. Alas, non-industrial fishing has lost out to foreign competition (English included) especially to Korea and Japan. The independent-minded Scottish National Party has put a claim on their territorial waters supporting small local fishing boats. They go out fishing and bring back a lot of…votes.

Finally, we come across Fraserburgh Promontory. Kinnaird Head Castle/Lighthouse is lit by its two hundred year old lighthouse. Northern Lighthouse has also taken over the castle which has been withstanding the wind since the sixteenth century. Its coast has no real natural harbors and plunges straight into a rough roaring sea.

ABOVE

The official capital of the Highlands, Inverness, lies at the center of a 100 kilometer circle allowing one to discover all the aspects of the Highlands.

RIGHT

Peterhead is the most important fishing port in Europe. Fish markets are at the center of the town which liven up at the end of each week when the fishing boats come in.

Dunnottar Castle, south of Stonehaven, was considered to be inaccessible. It's the last castle that stayed in the hands of the Royalists during the Protectorate in the seventeenth century. It was restored only in the beginning of the twentieth century.

LEFT

The small port of Stonehaven, south of Aberdeen, is sheltered from the winds coming in from the east northeast. It's an important center for training lifeboat teams.

The small ports on the east coast are also specialists in
prawns and lobster pots like here in Collieston.

*A panoramic view of the east and west of Tarbat ness on
the northeast coast of the Highlands.*

*Loch Firth, to the north of Inverness, is an important center
for construction and maintenance of off-shore platforms
between Nigg Yard and Invergordon.*

RIGHT

The bends of Wick River flowing into
the North Sea on the east coast.

Duncansby Head, at the extreme northeast of Scotland,
is a region suited for cereal agriculture.

Pentland Firth, the strait between
the Mainland and the Orkneys.

The Bay of Tongue offers the most beautiful
silver beaches on the north coast.

*The fishermen of the north coast don't hesitate to put
their pots at the foot of Cape Wrath.*

RIGHT

*Cape Wrath, the extreme northwest coast of the Highlands,
is the obligatory passage for fuel transport to the terminals
of the Orkneys and the Shetlands.*

*The Old Man of Hoy Island in the Orkneys is a gigantic needle
137 meters (449 feet) high. In the background, the cliff of
Saint John's Head plunging down 350 meters (1148 feet)
into the Atlantic Ocean.*

B ack to the helicopter, the motor of the Agusta 109 beats impatiently to get to the islands in the extreme north. They are called Orkneys and Shetlands. They count 90 islands on the port side and about a hundred on the starboard. There are about 17,000 inhabitants on the Orkneys and 19,000 on the Shetlands…Scattered over the big blue sea, they look like survivors from some kind of Atlantis. They are more spread out than the Hebrides. Because there is such a variety and multitude of rocky islands inhabited only by sterns, guillemots, and penguins, they are inaccessibly wild and unappealing to people. Wicked waves crash on their cliffs and currents whirl around them. Better give them a wide berth.

Wild and desolate, mauve and ashen, desert-like…the immense Sutherland, on the road to the isles looks this way from the sky. This land was snatched away from the inhabitants by the cynical expulsion decree made by the Earl of Sutherland (English) at the beginning of the nineteenth century.

The Earl of Sutherland was a ruthless man. His coat of arms represents a kind of wild cat, all claws out and saw-like teeth over a helmet and star filled shield…Even the last hamlet of the lowlands, from the vestiges of Hadrian's Wall, to the Lighthouse of Galway on the peninsula of Stranraer, to the extreme south of Scotland, forever remembers the tragic Clearances. The massive deportation of populations over the waters was not only a tragedy for the wandering Highlanders. Its memory – which inspired the "great exodus" of the French of Quebec to Louisiana – still moves people. The name Sutherland is part of that memory. Of the thousands of small farmers thrown out of the Sutherland, only a handful of shepherds are left, spread out in the rocky and windswept countryside.

Golspie is on the coastal route. And Dunrobin Castle.

Early morning on the cobblestone windy streets of Stromness.

Sutherland Castle, made up of 150 Baroque rooms, is nicknamed "Madness." It is compared to Louis II of Bavaria's castle. Every year in the month of August, the shepherd's dogs of the county are turned into competition dogs.

Helmsdale is also on the coast. The good Countess of Sutherland decreed that she would build a port for "her dear wanderers." The dispossessed farmers, who only knew how to catch river salmon, would now learn how to tame the waves!…She pushed them towards the imaginary port at sword point. The "herd" was therefore rounded up!

"Angus" is the breed of cattle in the Highlands. Sturdy and short, they give a particularly tender meat.

Second town of the Orkneys, Stromness is a fishing port where every house has its own boat launch.

They had marched all the way from Fort George, built by the English, right after Culloden. The fortress watched over Moray Firth in front of Inverness.

Some leagues from Helmsdale, the promised land, Philip makes a quick visit to Badbea, another Mecca of the outcasts. He peers across the desolate landscape, trying to fathom the story of the calamity in the ruins.

On the map, a neighboring name draws attention: *Navidade*, Christmas in Spanish. The vestiges of a vessel of the Invincible Armada still lies somewhere in the depths. That Christmas was a Requiem.

Finally, overlooking the water at the end of Sinclair County, the coat of arms which are the ermine and the heather cock, is the tip of this vertiginous country. John O'Groats doesn't owe his name to any of the Irish monks who were descendants of St. Colomba. The village attracted a Dutchman, Jan de Groot, who provided regular passage to the Orkneys.

After the beaches and white dunes of the Bay of Sinclair, the helicopter flies over the cliffs of pink stone at Duncansby Point. For a thrill, the helicopter flies really close to the Stacks, these needle-like rocks, standing as straight as a parade as though to salute the last stretch towards the isles.

"It's over, 'The last house of Scotland' is already behind us…"

"Ultima Thulé."

The ancients gave this name to the furthest land they could imagine to the north.

In 330 BC, it took the Greek explorer Pytheas about six days to sail to this hidden away scrap of land. Thulé was neither Iceland, nor was it the coast of Jutland or of Norway. Historians think that this bit of land might be part of the Shetlands, about 80 kilometers (49.7 miles) from the coast of Scotland.

As friendly rivals and neighbors lost in the sea, the inhabitants of the Orkneys – only one hour away by ferry from John O'Groats – also make their claim. Thulé? The immense rocky obelisk that comes out vertically on the west coast of the Isle of Hoy is all that is left of it. The Old Man of Hoy is 137 meters (449.4 feet) high, higher than the first floor of the Eiffel Tower. Facing the immense Atlantic, this is the last sentinel, a rocky watchtower, the last natural

monument of a forgotten land.

The line around the red cliffs stands out at sunset. There are only a few trees on the plateau even though the soil is good. Agriculture and sheep grazing are the activities there but also breeding of red longhaired cattle known as Highland cattle and especially short, robust ponies that are well known in the Shetlands.

West to Stromness. In the past this was a popular port where James Cook and other hardy sailors laid anchor. The sevententh cen-

tury was its time of glory as commerce had developed with the New World. In 1670, the Hudson Bay Company had set up its European headquarters there and in the year 1800, more than 500 employees, of which 400 came from the Orkneys via Stromness, worked in Canada. It is a 14 hour ferry ride from the port to the Shetlands.

Swinging across the most ecological golf course in the world, Philip looks dreamily, as all other sailors do, across the seas. The golf course of Stromness has a wonderful view across the ocean. It's the perfect place to try for a birdie or an eagle, a difficult thing to do here.

There are also the standing menhirs, *cairns* and *brochs* (circular towers) which take us back to the second millennium before Christ. The Ring of Brodgar was a perfect circle of 60 menhirs. Only half are left. They are more than 5 meters (16.4 feet) high. More ancient still, south of Berwick, lies a veritable necropolis from the Bronze Age. A farmer literally dug up the "tomb of the eagles" where, for 3000 years, 144 human remains had been buried! These "ends of the world" are archaeological and geological labyrinths as well as ornithological paradises. Photo safaris are organized there by the Royal Society for the Protection of Birds. Here, the prehistoric village suddenly appeared from under the sands like the site at Skara Brae which was suddenly unveiled by a storm in 1850. Out of nowhere, Viking treasures were discovered!

For five centuries, the Vikings had their claws on these islands. *Norn*, Nordic language, still competes with Gaelic. Scotland owes these maritime pearls to the marriage between James III and Margaret. Margaret was the daughter of the King of Norway and

in 1469 inherited these islands to her throne. Without her dowry, Scotland would have never produced whiskey on the islands. The highest distillery in Scotland – therefore of the world – is the pride of one of the Orkneys. Kirkwall has been the cradle since the French Revolution.

The Highland Park Distillery opens its doors to visitors who take the road to the south. You can recognize its two chimneys in the form of a pagoda covering its copper stills. Barley is imported, made into malt on the spot and dried on the iodine peat. They produce a dry and smoky malt. It can be drunk after it's been aged for 8 years. Its golden color turns to amber in 12 years. Connoisseurs prefer a limited edition, cask strength, when it is 14 or 24 years old.

Only 800 meters (half a mile) away, Scapa is its biggest competitor. To distinguish the second highest distillery in Scotland – thus in the world – is the northern specificity of the Orcades. Its label flaps over the sail of the Viking drakkar. Everything here, except the welcoming ritual of the bagpipes on the banks of Stromness, has a Scandinavian atmosphere. Norway, in a referendum, said "no" to joining the European Community. Here Norway finds a different way of being part of it. Many ships are anchored in the port of Kirkwall, in the Orkneys there are even more in the port of Lerwick, in the Shetlands. Many of them have Norwegian flags. Because of the "Viking Isles" the cargo-drakkars of the Norwegian merchant marine are able to sell their stocks to the continent. Food products made in Norway are processed in the local factories there. They come out labeled "made in the UK"…therefore made in Europe.

To see these islands transformed in this way inspires the locals this line, "More blond than red, more Nordic than Celtic,"

adding, "But the Norwegians are our brothers…" Christmas brings enlightening proof. They call Christmas, *up-Helly-A,* and in the Shetlands, parade horns replace the bagpipes of the Orkneys. Everywhere, from the mainland to the ultimate point of Sumburgh, to the south of the archipelago, and passing through the Viking sites of Jarlshof and the ruins of Scalloway Castle, torch-lit processions wind down to the sea. Even on the smallest fjord, peat fires burn, releasing an acrid smoke. The ritual is closed with a burning *drakkar* pushed out on to the waters.

Stromness port is alive day and night with its fish market and ferry terminal. A magnificent golf course is just to the south of the town and many ship crews go down to have a shot at the ball.

On the Isle of Eynballow, on the north of the archipelago, the ruins of the monastery da from the twelfth century.

The Ring of Brodgar and the Standing Stones (3000 BC). Originally 60 menhirs formed a perfect circle. Only 27 are left with a height going from 2 meters (6.5 feet) to 2 meters 50 (8.2 feet).

Skara Brae, on the west side of the Mainland. Houses dating from the Neolithic era.

Broch of Gurness, one of the most beautiful fortresses in the Orkneys, in the 1st century BC. The site was occupied until the ninth century.

Standing Stones of Stenness (3000 BC).
Originally this site was a cromlec'h of 12 menhirs.

The Hoy Sound is the stretch of sea that leads
to the Bay of Scapa on the Atlantic Ocean.
Squalls hit the Isle of Hoy.

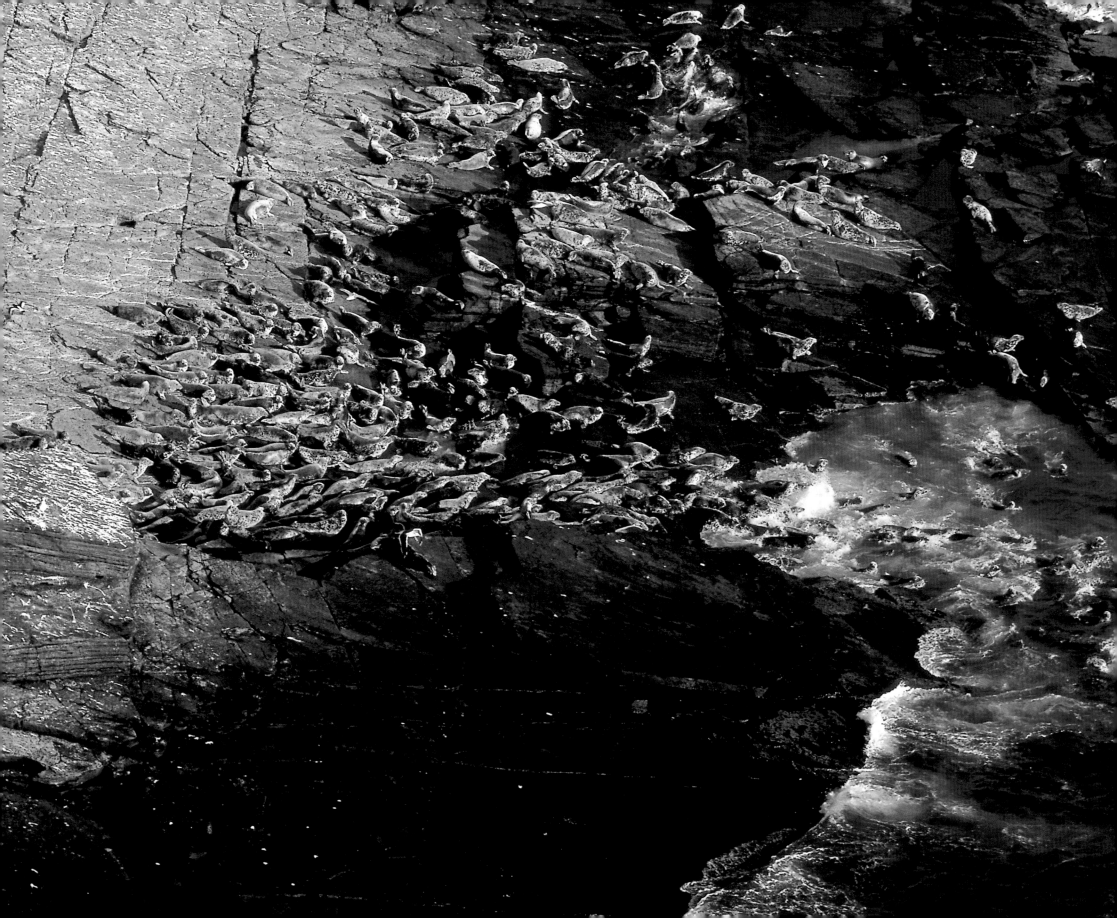

The herds of gray seals are estimated to be about 25,000
in the Orkneys archipelago. It is known that seals eat up to
5 kilos of fish a day. This is the reason
why fishing organizations take the problem very seriously.

RIGHT

More than a million birds nest on the Orkneys.
Three species have been found.

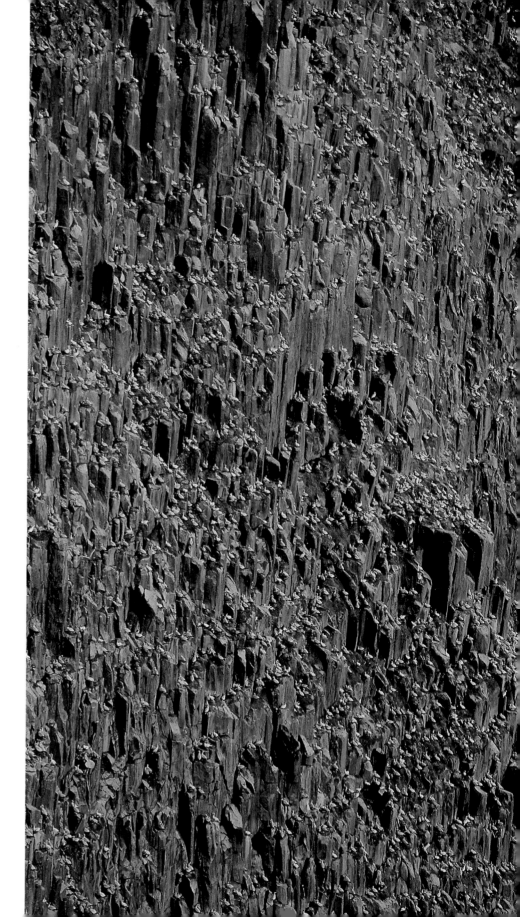

Fair Island.
Half way between the Orkneys and the Shetlands, this rock of 750 hectares (1853 acres) still shelters about twenty families who live from sheep and local craftwork intended for tourism.

On Fair Island, boats (in traditional shapes)
are laid out on the land for winter.

South Fair Island lighthouse was automated on
the 30th of March,1998 in the presence
of Princess Anne of England, patron of
Scottish Lighthouses and Beacons.
It was the last lighthouse to be run
by Great Britain.

*To the north of the Shetlands, Mackle Flugga, is the furthest
island from the United Kingdom. Its lighthouse was built
in 1854 by Thomas Stevenson and was automated in 1995.*

Jurassic Park, *20,000 Leagues Under the Sea* and *2001: A Space Odyssey*…The North Sea halfway between Scotland and Norway, offers a Hollywood-like field of exploration to researchers and to the seekers of black gold. British Petroleum is in competition with Elf, especially over these deposits where oil and gas lie in the depths of depths. Drilling is as deep as 1000 meters (3280 feet).

Since 1970, the Scottish have invested a big part of their future and semi-sovereignty on the exploitation of these oil fields. They are the largest reserves in Europe and Scotland is happy to have large steel platforms as big as flying saucers constructed over their ocean.

The 80 kilometers (49.71 miles) which separate the Orkneys from the Shetlands are scattered with massive constructions piercing the sea. Men live there on those fixed or floating platforms. They play at *breaking the waves*, tripling the salaries of their land based colleagues working in the refineries of the continent. The helicopters from Aberdeen, the biggest European fleet, picks the men up and

drops off their replacements, often for ten day or three week shifts.

Aberdeen, university town and industrial fishing port, has attracted a skilled population. Petrochemical engineers have created a new class. The old royal town is proud to be the "flower of Scotland." Thousands of rose bushes adorn the streets giving meaning to its title. With the sudden eruption of the oil industry, Aberdeen, the city of granite, loses its austerity and exhibits signs of new wealth.

One lives well in Aberdeen: well-dressed men, hip teenagers, chic women. Fashion City. Its motto: "A good alliance," which of course comes from the Franco-Scot *Auld Alliance*. It is a welcome sign for Elf.

The names of the company's drilling fields are Elgin and Franklin. Elgin, is at the same time the anagram for Nigel, a geologist and one of the pioneers of these deposits and also the name of a Gothic Cathedral of royal residence built in the thirteenth century and situated between Aberdeen and Inverness. The navigator, John Franklin, commanded the arctic expeditions of the nineteenth

The two jack ups of Elgin Franklin were constructed in Stornoway on Lewis Island in the Hebrides and were transported by barges to the gas fields 250 kilometers (155.3 miles) east of Aberdeen.

century. He opened the road to Alaska through the Strait of Davis in Greenland and by way of the northern tip of Canada. These names symbolized the foundations of a future, built on the certitude of a happy past and the present, upon a network of 473 kilometers (293.91 miles) of pipelines, 48,000 tons of construction, an investment of more than 2 billion dollars.

The vast zones of exploitation: the Hebrides, the Aberdeen region, Brent-Statfjord 250 kilometers (155.34 miles) north of the Shetlands, Frigg, 300 kilometers (186.41 miles) south of the Shetlands, Claymore Piper a little further out at sea from Wick, on the east coast of Sutherland. This is where Philip chooses to share life on board.

It's the oldest platform in Scotland. Here oil and gas are drilled. Claymore is built on jack ups. These pillars are drilled into the sea beds on which platforms are set. Its surface equals about 20 tennis courts. It covers 200 meters (656.1 feet) from the flame to the base. It's like an iron iceberg, leaving only a tenth of its mass visible, about 30 meters (98.42 feet) in all. This dimension allows Philip

to measure the strength of the storm which keeps him a prisoner for two days in Claymore. The wind is at 85 knots, about 150 kilometers (93.2 miles) an hour. The sky is white, the waves become heavy breakers. One crashes vertically onto the first platform, "Puq," used for production and supplies. The short shock is felt on the second platform. 120 men share their lives there. They are like a super team of lighthouse keepers…Even the jack ups tremble. The men who calculate the wind speed and know the measurements of the platform are specific. It's going to be a 25 meter (82 feet) wave. The next morning, at 6 o'clock, that's all they talk about in the cafeteria on board. And we know that these guys, huddled together on their steel island amidst the blue immensity, had seen others before it.

A little later, Philip learned, that a barge transporting a pipeline had lost its cargo in the storm. Six months later it was still being repaired…in Brest.

The 6th of July, 1998, the Piper Alfa platform caught on fire. 277 men died in the biggest catas-
trophe in the history of off-shore drilling. Today, the installations are separate:
on the one side, the extraction and the production units, and on the other linked by a walkway,
the living quarters, like here on the Claymore Cap.

The Elf terminal on the Isle of Flotta in the Orkneys archipelago is equipped with a buoy for loading fuel for the super tankers.

LEFT

More than two billion dollars has been invested in the Elgin Franklin. Together, the platform and the off-shore installations weigh 48,000 tons (compared to 33,000 tons for the French aircraft carrier Charles de Gaulle); The study and the construction of it took 3 years. It has also 473 kilometers (294 miles) of pipelines which equal 180,000 tons of steel and equals a 25 year supply for Gaz de France.

Back to the locks, more locks. Philip's trawler heads west. Closing the circle. With Inverness…Loch Ness…Loch Lochy…Fort William…Loch Linnhe…and finally back to Oban.

For the moment Philip Plisson abandons his boat on which he took images of his tour of Scotland from the North Sea. From now on it's by car. He drives down the A9 weaving between the mountains of Monadhilath and the peaks of Caingorm. The A9 goes through the Grampians, the Atholl forest and down to Edinburgh.

He stops at Pitlochry, at the gates of Perth, the town where the royal crowning took place. It is here that England stole the Stone of Scone, that medieval throne on which the kings of Scotland took their oath.

Around Blair Castle, people come here to hunt from all over the world. In Scotland, the art of hunting is a cultural sport. In the cold early morning, hunters meet up at the farm. The "hot whiskey," a blend with added cloves gets people going. Philip was brought up in the countryside of Sologne in France. It reminds him of the hunting rituals in his childhood.

In no time, they saddle up a pony and hook up a sulky. Up ahead, the pony boy gives his little foal a rest. He looks after it especially during the long waits for the stalker to find the best hunting site. The stalker sites his rifle and looks out to the red rocks and shrubs.

Suddenly, a herd emerges and splits up into small groups. About 100 wild deer running free. The rule is to be downwind. Like at sea. So, you walk and walk hoping to be well placed…"Lie down and don't move. Hide," commands the stalker. Suddenly, he whispers, "There it is!" The target of the day is identified due to the deer antlers. This is how he proceeds. The first rule is to identify which deer to shoot and the second rule, kill it. This time it's going to be a ten pointer. It's ten years old and they've been looking for it for a long time. Bounding through the grass, he invites the hunters to follow. The hunter points his gun from behind a curtain of leaves. Third rule: the hunter is only allowed two bullets.

There is an abundance of deer in the Highlands, about 300,000 head. Every year, the Reed Deer Commission determines the number that have to be killed. The deer is still considered to be a nuisance in certain areas.

The deer falls with the first shot. The others scatter. In a few minutes, the hunters run down the hill towards the dead animal. Without a word and out of respect, they contemplate their prey. It looks beautiful and brave as it lays frozen in a deathly stupor. The stalker takes a blade out of his pocket. Immediately he bleeds the animal and with a vivid gesture cuts off the testicles in order to prevent the deer's upper thighs from being covered in urine.

The hunters form a small circle. They take out their little bottles of whiskey, salmon or dried meat sandwiches and reminisce about their hunting stories for about an hour in the clear air. A simple nodding of the head signals that it's time to go back. The knives are cleaned, folded back and the pony boy packs the game on the saddle. It takes years to train a pony to tolerate an animal on its back. The strong smell of blood makes it instinctively want to escape from it.

At five o'clock, the hunters head back to the village. The butcher is already there. He carves up the deer straight away. During a simple ritual they make a symbolic offering of the horns and ten antlers. They clink their single malts (from the region) and dream of more long walks and hunting days.

But Philip will never forget the soft setting sun on the east coast. Comfortably settled in a hotel room (usually converted castles from the past), he feels that he's being watched.

The television is on. Already, the shadow of a Scottish ghost is in his thoughts. Slowly, Philip turns around. A deer, probably escaped from the neighboring forests, has come to graze on the bit of freshly mown lawn. Attracted by the light in the room, its head is almost leaning on the window ledge. His two horns stand out in the frame. He seems to be staring at the multi-colored action of a football match on the TV screen. Philip doesn't have his camera ready. The soft look on the deer's eyes will forever be fixed in his memory.

This sport is a passion. This kind of traditional
deer hunting is done in the Highlands.
The stalker leads the hunt, chooses the animal
and organizes the approach.

Dundee is only an arm's length away from Perth. A visit there is a must for those who are interested in Amundsen. It was here, around 1900, that the explorer prepared his expeditions to the poles…until his last tragic trip, in 1928. Everywhere, sailboats glide like swans. The specialty in the area is marmalade… from breakfast to tea time. This sweet was invented by a local grocer upset that he had gotten a stock of rotten oranges from Spain! Linen is a local industry. Sails and sailor's coats are made by local weavers who have made their fortune with it.

To the north, Arbroath is camped on the white cliffs which drop vertically into the sea. Robert Bruce signed the Declaration of Independence of Scotland in his abbey in 1320 and proclaimed himself sovereign of the new kingdom.

To the south, Saint Andrews, the "Mecca of golf:" the old religious capital faces the sea and the western sandy beaches where the film *Chariots of Fire* was shot. It's on these dunes that idle shepherds killed time by hitting rocks with their shepherd sticks. They were trying to get the rocks into rabbit holes, thus inventing the art of putting! Marie Stuart gave her blessing to what would become the "sport of kings." The old course of St. Andrews, created in 1774, competes with Edinburgh (also 1774) for the crown of the oldest golf course in the world.

Going into Edinburgh from the bay of St. Andrews is more picturesque by the coast. It's full of little ports. In the small port of Kilconquhar, near the Scottish Fishing Museum, Philip Plisson has fun negotiating a case of freshly caught lobsters. The fisherman tips his cap and mumbles a price: 5 pounds (8 dollars)! Four times less the kilo than the lobster bought on fishing trawlers.

Edinburgh is the capital. Essentially, it's a rock crowned by a castle 133 meters (436.3 feet) above sea level. The town was built in the middle of an extinct volcano. That's where its Gaelic name comes from: Dun Edin, "the fort on the mountain." The cannon is fired every day, except Sunday – *Sunday is closed*. The Mons Meg dates from 1449 and weighs 5 tons. It was capable of firing a cannonball three kilometers (1.86 miles).

During Edinburgh's summer festival, "Amazing Grace" is played by bagpipes of the Highlands on the castle towers while the

curtain falls on the annual parade of the Military Tattoo. Edinburgh is Scotland's showcase. Scotland of yesterday and tomorrow. The Royal Scots Dragons seem to mount an eternal guard. Walter Scott, Robert Byrne, and Robert Louis Stevenson have written their works here. The Royal Mile runs down medieval streets, Princess Street opens up on to gardens, the Georgian houses of Charlotte Square, the treasures of its museums and painting galleries, all give Edinburgh its superior aristocratic style.

To the east, the port of Leith, where so many royal visitors land. The Duke of Edinburgh, Queen Elizabeth, and Princess Anne have their Scottish residences there at Holyrood Palace in the south. Here, Stevenson wrote, "these walls have been witness to conspiracies of war, and pacts of love and death."

There is another palace, half-noble, half-popular. It's the open roofed pagan temple in the Murrayfield neighborhood. It's the temple of rugby. Everyone puffs up with fervor, piety and pride, especially when the *Rose of England* rubs against the *Fifteen Thistles*.

Bagpipes and drums of the 51st Highlands Brigade sound *Scotland the Brave* while they attack. The stadium rocks. The fans quiver. Against all rules of protocol, loud noise covers *God Save the Queen...*

The crowd becomes ecstatic when the Pipe Major, Ryan Kerr (same name as Jim Kerr, the singer of Simple Minds) and Kenneth Davidson, the Trombone Major, start to play the first slow and majestic notes of "Flower of Scotland."

*O flower of Scotland
When will we see you like again
That fought and died for
Your wee bit hill and glen
And stood against him
Proud Edward's army
And sent him homeward
(…)*

*Those days are passed now
And in the past they must remain
But we can still rise now
And be a nation again
That stood against him
Proud Edward's army
And sent him homeward.*

When in 1974, Roy Williamson, the singer of the Corries, wrote these lyrics, he didn't know that he was giving Scotland its modern national anthem. 60,000 copies of the sheet music are distributed on the day of the match.

When the Scots nail the English on their line in the big match and score the winning try, it's revenge for Rob Roy, William Wallace – *Braveheart* – there's a quasi-religious clamor in the stadium.

In the pubs of Edinburgh, in the Malt Shovel or the Queen's

Arms (Mary, Queen of Scotland), the violins are out. So is the kileann pipe and the bodhran (a tambourine played with a stick). The beer flows, amber beer, and like drunken sailors the crowd gets carried away by the froth. Edinburgh has numerous festivals, it's especially famous for The Edinburgh Summer Festival in August. In 1999, the Scottish Parliament reopened its doors. Until 1640, it used to meet in the large halls of the castle over the old jails, "the French prison." This is where the King of France's soldiers were taken prisoners having fought in the name of the *Auld Alliance*.

In the era of the euro and Euroland, we can understand why Scotland is so proud to print out its own currency, the bluenotes signed, "Bank of Scotland."

Around Edinburgh, lie the Borders, the Lowlands surrounded by low hills. When he came back from Cornwall, Wales and the Isle

of Man in the fifth century, armed with Excalibur, his golden sword, King Arthur liked to rest here. He went to the top of Eildan Hills to survey his Celtic kingdom. In the west, he looked onto the coasts of Ireland from the Stanraer Peninsula.

Philip Plisson sails out to sea between the two coasts. He bids farewell to Scotland before he heads off for Dublin and then down to Cork.

The Emerald Isle by the blue waters.

RIGHT
Edinburgh Festival closes with a gigantic fireworks display over the castle.

Edinburgh seen from up high is very beautiful like here at the bottom of the National Monument looking down Princes Street.

Edinburgh is a "permanent festival."
All year round, the town welcomes
many artistic and cultural activities.

RIGHT

In the past, the port of Leith was
closely associated with Bordeaux wine.
As early as the fifteenth century,
French wine had an important place
in all social classes. Today, Leith,
a suburb of Edinburgh, is alive with
more and more quality pubs
and restaurants along the banks.

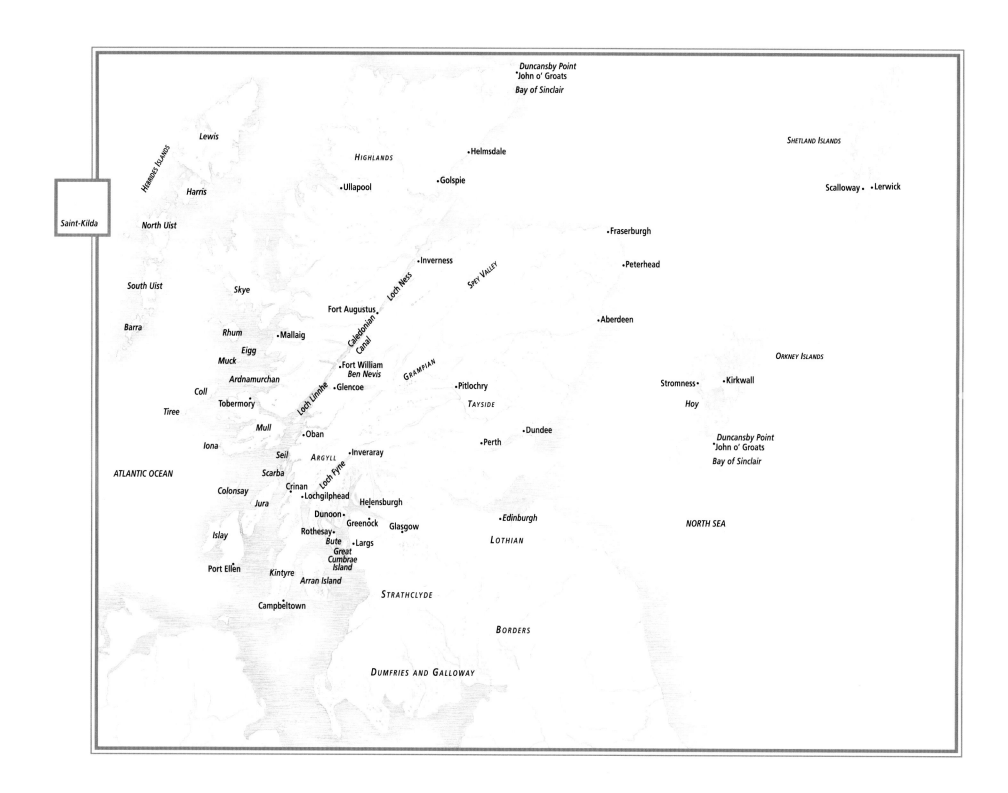

Duncansby Point
John o' Groats
Bay of Sinclair

HIGHLANDS

•Helmsdale

SHETLAND ISLANDS

Lewis

HEBRIDES ISLANDS

Harris

•Golspie

•Ullapool

Scalloway • • Lerwick

Saint-Kilda

North Uist

•Fraserburgh

South Uist

Skye

•Inverness

•Peterhead

Loch Ness

SPEY VALLEY

Barra

Fort Augustus•

•Aberdeen

Rhum

•Mallaig

Caledonian Canal

ORKNEY ISLANDS

Eigg
Muck

Fort William•

Ardnamurchan

Ben Nevis

GRAMPIAN

Stromness• •Kirkwall

Coll

Loch Linnhe

•Glencoe

•Pitlochry

Hoy

Tobermory•

Tiree

TAYSIDE

Mull

•Oban

•Dundee

Duncansby Point
John o' Groats
Bay of Sinclair

Iona

•Inveraray

Seil

ARGYLL

•Perth

Scarba

Loch Fyne

ATLANTIC OCEAN

Crinan

Colonsay

•Lochgilphead

Helensburgh

Jura

Dunoon•

•Edinburgh

NORTH SEA

Rothesay•

Greenock

Glasgow

Islay

Bute

•Largs

LOTHIAN

Great
Cumbrae
Island

Port Ellen

Kintyre

Arran Island

STRATHCLYDE

Campbeltown•

BORDERS

DUMFRIES AND GALLOWAY

Recommended reading material

TRIPS

Pictures from Scotland,
Karl Johaentges, Jackie, Blackwood, éd. Kajo
Écosse, les secrets des Highlands,
Sébastian Thewes and Yves Gellié, éd. Casterman
Écosse,
Kenneth White, Erwan Quémeré, éd. Arthaud
Terre d'Écosse,
Serge Olério and Stéphanie Grandval, éd. Barthélémy
Écosse,
under the direction of Kenneth White,
with the participation of Michel Le Bris and
Jacques Darras, éd. Autrement.
Écosse, Highlands et Islands,
Michel Le Bris, éd. Artus
Saint-Kilda, Tom Steel, éd. Peuples du monde

HISTORY

Scotland's Glory,
Patrick Laughlin, éd. Jarrold Publishing
The Jacobites,
Antony Kamm, édition Scotties books
Culloden, 1746, The Highland Clan's Last Charge
Peter Harrington, éd. Osprey
Flora Mac Donald, the Highland Heroine,
éd. Jarrold Publishing

Mary Queen of Scots, éd. Jarrold Publishing
Scottish Clans, éd. Pitkin guide
Scottish Tartans, éd. Pitkin guide
Bonnie Prince Charlie, éd. Pitkin guide

GUIDES

Orkney, Patrick Bailey, éd. Pevensey guide
Écosse, Guides Bleus Évasion, éd. Hachette
Écosse, le Guide du Routard, éd. Hachette
Le guide des gréements, éd. Le Chasse-Marée
Une semaine en Écosse,
collection Marco Polo, éd. Hachette

WHISKEY

Le Whisky sans peine,
Jean Pierre Pichard, éd. Coop Breizh
La Magie du whisky,
Patrick Mahé and David Lefranc, Éd. du Chêne

BIRDS

Puffins,
Roy Dennis, éd. Colin Baxter
Les oiseaux de mer,
Philippe Moteau and Philippe Garguil,
éd. Jean Paul Gisserot

BIOGRAPHY

R. L. Stevenson,
Michel Le Bris, éd. Nil

ESSAYS

La course aux trésors,
Jean de Kerdeland, éd. S.P.I.E.

MUSIC

La musique celtique,
Didier Convenant, éd. Hors Collection

SPORT

Génération Supporter,
Philippe Broussard, éd. Robert Laffont

MAPS

Scotland, touring map, éd. Bartholomew
Clan map, éd. Bartholomew

MAGAZINES

L'interceltique, Lorient
Artus, La Gacilly
Loch Ness,
booklet on the film by John Henderson

Useful addresses

Terre d'Écosse   135, avenue de Wagram 75017 Paris
Tel. : 01 47 57 31 32
Fax : 01 47 58 41 14

La Maison du Whisky   20, rue d'Anjou 75008 Paris
Tel. : 01 42 65 03 16

The Auld Alliance   80, rue François Mirron 75004 Paris
Tel. : 01 42 04 30 40

Festival Interceltique   2, rue Paul Bert 56100 Lorient
Tel. : 02 97 21 24 29
Fax : 02 97 64 34 13

Acknowledgements

Jonathan Findlay (Terre d'Écosse),
Michel Le Bris,
Jean-Pierre Pichard,
Martine Mac Mahé,
"Magic" Mick Gerriet

The 29th of July, 1998, in Trinité-sur-Mer channel, my eyes could have closed forever.
Of course, the women and men who had accompanied me in the adventure of this book
would have seen that this work would be completed.
My friend, Patrick Mahé, would have found beautiful words to speak about my last look onto
this world that I have loved so much.
It would have been moving…
But this last page would have been probably missing, my sincere thanks, and,
I am very happy tonight to be able to thank them myself.

To those who have believed in my project:
And in particular to Isabelle Jendron, General Director of Chêne Publishing
Thank you to those who have given me the means to reach my dreams:
The President of Elf Aquitaine, to his department of communications and to the staff of Elf
UK in Aberdeen.
Thank you to those who accompanied on my voyage:
Antonia Small, the small American from Massachusetts who came to be reinvigorated on the
Highlands and Christophe Le Potier, my assistant.
Thank you to those who supplied transportation over the channel:
The commanders of the Bretagne of Brittany Ferries and their crew.
Thank you to those who guided us above these ends of the world:
Michael Marlie-Smith of Casterl Air and the crews of Bond Helicopters.
Thank you to those who warmly welcomed us:
My friend Neil Corbasson, Lorna Grieve and the crews of the N.L.B. (Scottish Lighthouse
and Beacons).
Thank you to those who followed the weather forecasts:
The maritime forecaster of Météo France in Toulouse and the services of Météo Fax.
Thank you to those who have edited this book:
The team from Vu par… in Nantes.
Thank you to those who printed this book:
Master printer Jean-Paul Le Govic and his team in Nantes.
Finally, thank you to those who have taken the time to turn these pages. I have lent you my
eyes on my simple voyage and I hope that through my vision, lovers of Scotland will
rediscover the atmosphere that they hold so dearly in their hearts.

Photographically yours,

La Trinité-sur-Mer, October 10, 1998

www.plisson.com – email: philip@plisson.com

The photos in this were taken with Canon (EOS 1N & Series L) cartridges
and optical lenses, the panoramic photos with FUJI 6x17.
The ensemble of the work was shot with
FUJIchrome 135 & 220 film, with the exception of the photo on page 88
taken out at sea from Scotland by Didier Peyron,
chief mechanic on board the Pétrel.

Publishing
Valérie Tognali and Cécile Aoustin

Paste-up
Vu par…, Nantes

Binding
SMRF, Muzillac

Photoengraving :
Le Govic, Nantes – France

Printing :
Toppan Printing Co., Hong Kong

First published in France in 1998 by Editions du Chêne-Hachette Livre.
Copyright © 1998 Editions du Chêne-Hachette Livre. All rights reserved.

'This edition first published in the UK in 2003 by Hachette Illustrated
UK, Octopus Publishing Group Ltd., 2-4 Heron Quays, London E14 4JP

Reprinted in 2004